Home Buying
by the EXPERTS™

The Pros Make Your Dream Home a Reality

D1510157

Brian Yui and Lori Shaw-Cohen

QUANTUM
LEAVES
PUBLISHING

Copyright © 2005 by Quantum Leaves Publishing℠

This publication is designed to provide accurate and authoritative information in regard to the subject matter covered. It is sold with the understanding that the publisher is not engaged in rendering legal, accounting, or other professional service. If legal advice or other expert assistance is required, the services of a competent professional person should be sought.

—*From a declaration of principles jointly adopted by a committee of the American Bar Association and a committee of publishers*

ISBN 0-9761526-0-6

Quantum Leaves Publishing is a division of MBA Commercial, Inc. Quantum Leaves Publishing's books and products are available by special order through most bookstores or on the Internet at www.quantumleaves.com. To contact Quantum Leaves Publishing directly, call 888.248.6222 or email info@quantumleaves.com.

Substantial discounts on bulk quantities of Quantum Leaves Publishing books are available to corporations, professional associations, and other organizations. For details and discount information, contact the special sales department at Quantum Leaves Publishing.

First Edition. Printed in the United States of America.

Published by Quantum Leaves Publishing℠
Del Mar, California.
www.quantumleaves.com

Credits on page 207

Special Thanks

Eric Berman and Jim Bunch for their contacts and assistance

Ellen Stiefler for the legalese

"The Street Kid" for his good advice

Audrey Adams and Robert Polgar for their artistic guidance

All our wonderful experts for imparting their wisdom, years of experience and tips of the trade to home buyers everywhere

Herb Tanzer for his enlightened point of view

Tracy Stevens for her diligence and valuable "two cents"

Bob for his reliable feedback and devotion

Jessica, Joshua, Drew and Logan for their never-ending inspiration and motivation

Contents

Foreword
~∞ Lori Shaw-Cohen, Writer & Editor

Know Your Home Buying Potential
~∞ Brian Yui, CEO HouseRebate.com

The ABCs of Financing Your Home
~∞ William Emerson, CEO Quicken Loans

Finding Your Ideal Home
ᴑᴑ Brian Yui, CEO HouseRebate.com

How to Buy Property with No Money Down
ᴑᴑ Robert G. Allen, Author of "Nothing Down" & Other Best-Sellers

Winning Bidding Strategies
ᴑᴑ Brian Yui, CEO HouseRebate.com

What to Expect from Your Home Inspection
∼◌ Keith S. Fimian, Chairman & Founder U.S. Inspect, LLC

From Contract to Closing
∼◌ Stewart Morris, Jr., President & CEO Stewart Title Company

Moving Made Easy
∼◌ Michael P. Fergus, President SIRVA Global Moving Services (Retired)

Reap the Rewards: Tax Benefits

∽ōō Robert J. Bruss, Tax Specialist & Real Estate Columnist

Setting Goals to Buy the Home of Your Dreams

∽ōō Brian Tracy, Motivational Speaker & Best-Selling Author

Home Buying Highlights

Resources

Foreword

Lori Shaw-Cohen

When Brian Yui, CEO of HouseRebate.com and my childhood friend of 30 years, first approached me with his idea for *Home Buying by the Experts*, I knew immediately it was a winner. After all, seeking advice from those in the know on things we don't understand is a natural inclination. Whether it's home buying, cooking, computer technology or the stock market, most of us turn to professionals to teach us what we need to learn. In this book, we round up the pros and bring them to you!

I had been working on an installment of my weekly newspaper column when Brian and I began brainstorming about the book. As a wife of almost a quarter century and mother of three, I primarily write about family issues and as luck or fate would have it, I had recently been reflecting on life as a new wife all those years ago. That was a time of "firsts"—our first anniversary, first car, first baby and of course, our first home.

Like many young couples beginning their lives together, my husband and I rented a house for a couple of years. Before long, however, we were ready to explore homes we could afford to buy. We had become frustrated watching our substantial rent payment disappear every month and longed to paint a wall, hang a picture and change a fixture without permission from an omnipresent landlord.

Unsure where to begin, my husband called a client who was an experienced and successful local real estate agent. He trusted her to abide by our budget and understand that, as a young couple, God willing, we'd have babies—and extra bedrooms—in our future.

After wading through piles of spec sheets and walking through many "No ways!" we found our gem amidst the rubble. It was a fixer-upper, but it had personality, property and potential! It also had a slightly higher price tag than our finances would allow. Nevertheless, we listened carefully to our patient agent explain the etiquette of negotiation until our heads felt like they might explode.

Luckily, my husband's mother and stepdad were real estate agents in Pennsylvania, so we burned up the telephone wires from Southern California to Philadelphia, seeking protocol, discussing strategies and trying to learn everything we could before someone scooped up the prize before us.

There was so much to know! Like a too-low ceiling fan, we kept bumping into unfamiliar real estate terms: title insurance, loan points, counter offers, escrow. It was like learning a foreign language.

With the help of my in-laws and our agent, we plodded through and eventually got the property. The sellers were highly motivated (translation: close to foreclosure). According to many friends and acquaintances, we were lucky: We had a team of trusted relatives who knew the ins and outs of home buying and an agent who genuinely cared.

While working on this book, it made me think about all the people—young and old, couples with children, singles and newly married couples—who've scrimped and saved. Like us, many didn't know about the daunting home buying journey they were about to embark upon. How many homeowners (first-timers and veterans alike!) learned in hindsight, after spending too much, researching too little or choosing the wrong loans, that they'd made costly and long-term mistakes?

Even, years later, as more "savvy" homeowners, we made several buying blunders when we bought our second house in Nashville. Creative financing seemed more prevalent, tax laws had been updated, more loan options became available and of course, terms and procedures sometimes varied from state to state. My husband and I did what this book warns against: We trusted the wrong realtor, chose an inexperienced inspector and missed out on many tax deductions. Furthermore, house hunting on the Internet wasn't yet the incredible tool it is today; if it had been, we would have investigated more areas and homes in our price range. Even as I compiled and edited these chapters I realized how much I still didn't know. (I'll be prepared, though, when it's time to purchase my "empty-nest home" in the near future!)

So, as I tell my kids, learn from my mistakes! Consider *Home Buying by the Experts* not only advice from leading authorities in the real estate field, but also counsel from friends. Friends who care enough to help you avoid the many pitfalls and expensive mistakes that buying a home can present and make the best choices for your particular circumstances.

And, don't worry if you're not sure that home ownership is something you're ready for or able to do. Our experts can help you figure that out, too. World-renown motivational speaker and best-selling author Brian Tracy helps you plan for your future home in "Setting Goals to Buy the Home of Your Dreams" and my pal Brian walks you through the formula that'll help you determine if you can afford that home now in "Know Your Home Buying Potential." The path leading to your new front door is closer than you might think!

Good luck on your journey. I'm confident that with *Home Buying by the Experts* and a little faith, your dream home is out there waiting just for you!

Know Your Home Buying Potential

Brian Yui
CEO, HouseRebate.com

Shelter is a basic necessity and everyone needs housing in some shape or form. Owning a home, whether it's a "starter" or a dream home is a goal shared by millions. The good news is that today, it's easier to buy a home than ever before. Loan programs have become more readily available, terms are negotiable and numerous creative ways to circumvent a large down payment are often possible. In fact, sometimes it takes less cash to buy a home than it does to rent an apartment!

Whether you're a first-time home buyer or a seasoned veteran, there are home-purchasing fundamentals that every consumer should know. Within these pages, you will find the advice of real estate experts on every step leading to the front door of your dream home. The contributing authorities in the real estate field provide you with the knowledge and tips of the trade that come from years of experience. In other words, in your hands you hold the road map to make the home buying hassle a thing of the past.

Reasons to Rent

Most of us rent prior to buying a home. Eventually, most renters strive to purchase property, not only as the realization of a long-time dream, but also as an excellent investment and hedge against inflation.

Depending upon your circumstances, there are both pros and cons to renting. As a renter, you need a security deposit but not a down payment or long-term financial commitment. You also have the flexibility to change residences with few costs other than moving expenses.

In higher priced areas, renting may even be less expensive than buying. For example, a $100,000 home may rent for about $800 a month, but a $500,000 home will likely rent for considerably less than $4,000 a month. Rent does not go up proportionally with the price of the home.

 If you can't afford to buy in the area of your choice, rent there and buy a rental unit in an area you can afford.

Renters Avoid Additional Expenses

When deciding whether to rent or buy, the first step is to weigh the cost of home ownership against the cost of renting. For instance, your landlord uses a portion of your rent payment to cover certain housing expenses (see below). When you decide to purchase a home, you accept responsibility for the payment of these expenses in addition to your monthly mortgage cost, so they should be incorporated into your budget estimates.

The expenses may include:

- Property Taxes and Special Assessments
- Home/Hazard Insurance
- Utilities
- Maintenance (landscaping, wear and tear, painting, etc.)
- Homeowner's Association Fee (HOA) (usually covers trash and maintenance of common grounds and exterior of buildings)
- Membership Fee (pays for recreational facilities and services such as cable TV)

Reasons to Buy

Home ownership provides excellent tax and investment benefits. In the United States, home mortgage interest and property taxes are usually tax-deductible, which may result in considerable savings. While it's wise to consult a real estate professional, tax specialist or investment advisor about your specific situation, see "Reap the Rewards: Tax Benefits" beginning on page 83 for more from our tax expert.

As housing prices rise, homeowners can reap the benefits of selling or staying in the home and paying a fixed mortgage while rents continue to increase in the same neighborhood. If the value of your home increases to the point where you can sell it for more than your purchase price, that difference in value is called "appreciation." If you choose to sell your home, you can reinvest the profits in other real estate or downsize and bank that money for retirement or other purposes.

When you own your home, you are paying rent to yourself instead of a landlord. Most homeowners pay for property by obtaining a mortgage; as they pay off that mortgage, they gain an increasingly larger share in a valuable asset. The best way to look at it is like a forced savings plan. When your mortgage is paid off, you will obtain more net proceeds when you sell your home.

Another advantage to owning a home is that you are not beholden to a landlord. To begin with, you aren't subject to rent increases or eviction. You're free to redecorate and remodel to suit your lifestyle and taste and choose your own contractors without the property owner's permission. The benefits of home ownership are not only that you have the right to make improvements, but also that the value of those improvements becomes yours.

Ultimately, the greatest reward is the pride that comes from owning your own home. Few accomplishments in life are as enduring or enriching as the experience of owning a home. Nevertheless, carefully weigh the pros and cons of both renting and purchasing before making any decisions.

A Few More Facts About Renting vs. Buying

- If paying rent saves 35% or more versus the costs of owning (mortgage, insurance, taxes, maintenance, etc.), renting is generally a better option.

- When determining the costs of owning, remember that the interest paid on a mortgage is tax-deductible up to one million dollars. Calculate the after-tax expenditure of purchasing a home versus the after-tax costs of renting a home.

- The financial benefits of owning a home, including mortgage interest tax deduction and capital gain realized from the sale of the home, can offset the total costs of home ownership.

- If you have past credit problems that remain on your record, it may be wise to rent until the issues are resolved. Otherwise, mortgage rates might be too high and the amount you can borrow may be limited. There are companies that can assist you in correcting credit issues.

- It's usually a bad idea to buy a house that you will own for less than four years; costs of selling and buying are high, so if the home's value does not appreciate adequately before you sell, the consequence could be a net loss. Obviously, the exception to this is if your area is experiencing rapid growth and dramatic appreciation.

 Homes within good school districts tend to increase in value more reliably.

Here's another look at the pros and cons of both renting and buying.

Renting Advantages:
- ✓ Minimum liability
- ✓ Freedom to move without having to sell first
- ✓ Little responsibility for maintenance
- ✓ Security deposit vs. down payment

Renting Disadvantages:
- ✗ No control over rent increases
- ✗ Landlord can evict
- ✗ No equity or tax deductions
- ✗ All improvements must be approved by landlord

Buying Advantages:
- ✓ Accrued capital gain when you sell
- ✓ Tax benefits
- ✓ Pride of ownership
- ✓ Freedom to renovate
- ✓ No landlord to raise rent or evict

Buying Disadvantages:
- ✗ Less mobility
- ✗ Responsibility for expenses (i.e. insurance, property tax, HOA fees, repairs, etc.)
- ✗ Transactional costs when you sell (brokers' commissions, closing costs)
- ✗ Risk of foreclosure if unable to make payments
- ✗ Home value subject to market fluctuations

There are several "Rent vs. Buy Calculators" available on the Internet, including the one below from the Department of Housing and Urban Development.

Buying vs. Renting

	Rent	Buy
Current Rent		$1000
Purchase Price of Home:		$250,000
Percentage of Down Payment:		10%
Length of Loan Term (years):		30
Interest Rate:		7.5%
Years You Plan to Stay in This Home:		10
Yearly Property Tax Rate:		1.25%
Yearly Home Value Increase Rate:		3%
Result Returned	**Rent**	**Buy**
Price of Home After Appreciation:		$335,979
Remaining Balance After 10 Years:		$193,239
Equity Earned:		$142,740
Tax Savings (at 28%):	$1,113	$25,850
Avg. Monthly Payment Over Time:	$133,560	$640
Total Payment		$76,913
Total Savings On:	Buying: $69,062	

Note: The calculator above uses these items in its calculations: private mortgage insurance, homeowner's insurance cost, loan closing cost, cost of selling a home, property tax, homeowner's tax saving, and rent increases.

A Realistic Approach to Home Buying

In order to determine your home buying ability, a review of your income, savings, monthly expenses and debt will be necessary. These criteria will give you a better idea of what you can afford and how your monthly budget will be affected by purchasing a home. Take a look at your finances and lifestyle using the criteria below.

Income

The key to your home buying potential is your income. A mortgage is a long-term commitment and it helps to look not only at your cash flow today, but also to consider the future.

- What is your average monthly income?
- Is your income stable?
- Are any increases or decreases in income anticipated in the near future?

Savings

When buying a home, there are some costs that you cannot finance through your loan such as insurance and property tax that are due and payable at closing. Estimate your monthly savings by examining your habits, accounts, retirement fund, mutual fund investments, stocks and any other savings.

- How much of your income are you currently saving?
- Can you put away more money?

Added Monthly Expenses

Ask yourself honestly if you can afford an increase in monthly expenses. If saving is a problem for you now, your finances might be too tight to purchase a home.

- How will your monthly budget be affected?
- Can you handle any additional expenses that buying a home will necessitate?

Use the chart below to help estimate your current monthly costs and determine how buying a home might impact your budget.

Monthly Expenses	Current
Alimony/Child Support	$
Car Expenses	$
Clothing/Personal Items	$
Entertainment	$
Insurance	$
Medical Expenses	$
Taxes	$
Utilities	$
Total	$

Debt

House payments in addition to your existing debt can dramatically affect your lifestyle. Make a list of all current monthly debt and expenses to decide if you can afford more.

- Will the amount of debt you have compared to your income influence a lender's decision to grant your mortgage amount?
- How much more debt can you realistically manage?
- Will you be able to cover your debt through the life of your loan?

The Bottom Line

Most lenders prefer that homeowners have at least three months of living expenses available after closing on a loan. After all monthly costs and living expenses have been paid, how much cash and savings do you have left?

Keep in mind that closing costs, which generally depend upon the location of the house, type of loan and amount of down payment, will have to be paid.

 Sometimes a buyer can negotiate closing costs with the seller and lenders and/or finance a portion of the closing costs as part of the loan amount.

The truth is that most people can afford a house valued at roughly 2 1/2 times their gross annual salary. Individual circumstances vary and can alter this estimate in either direction. For instance, if you have more money available for a down payment, a more expensive house may be manageable because your mortgage payments will be smaller. Or, low interest rates may encourage you to buy a higher priced home while high interest rates may limit what you can afford. Generally, lenders will allow you to pay no more than 29% of your gross salary toward your mortgage while keeping monthly debt payments to about 41% or less of your gross income.

Don't be discouraged; there is a home out there that fits both your needs and your budget. Our experts are here to show you the way.

The ABCs of Financing Your Home

William Emerson
CEO, Quicken Loans

For many first-time home buyers, the word "mortgage" causes nervousness and anxiety, but home financing doesn't have to be difficult. With a little preparation and a basic understanding of how the mortgage process works, applying for a mortgage and closing your loan will be easy and stress-free.

What is a Mortgage?

Unless you have enough money to pay for a house yourself (and the vast majority of Americans do not) you'll need a mortgage. A mortgage is a loan you take out to finance the purchase of your home. It's also a legal contract stating that you promise to make a monthly payment until your loan is paid off.

There are several ways to secure a mortgage. You can get one directly by working with a mortgage banker or you can go to a bank, credit union or savings and loan. Today, there are more than 40,000 lending entities in the United States. Some are very small companies and may originate loans only for people in a particular state. Others, like Quicken Loans, are large companies that work with people all over the country.

Generally speaking, larger companies will have a broader array of mortgage programs from which to choose. It isn't uncommon for a large lender to have more than 100 different mortgage programs. A reputable industry professional can help you determine which mortgage program is best for your particular situation. That person should also provide you with advice throughout the entire loan process.

Mortgage Rates

Before taking a look at your mortgage options, it's important that you understand mortgage rates and points.

Think of your mortgage rate as the interest rate, or fee, you're charged to borrow money from your lender. Mortgage rates are tied to a particular economic index such as the London Interbank Offering Rate (LIBOR) or the value of the 10-year Treasury Bill. How your mortgage rate moves up or down—or whether it moves at all—will depend upon the mortgage program you select.

For example, with a fixed-rate program your interest rate is fixed for the entire term of your loan. In contrast, with an adjustable-rate mortgage, your rate is fixed for a period of time—usually one, three, five or seven years—and then changes based on the index to which it's tied. (Fixed-rate mortgages and adjustable-rate mortgages are explained in greater detail later on in this chapter.)

The rate on your mortgage is expressed as a percentage and interest accumulates over time on the unpaid balance of your loan. The higher your mortgage rate, the larger your monthly mortgage payment. Keep in mind, however, that unlike the interest you pay on a credit card, the interest you pay on your home loan may be tax-deductible. This is one of the reasons that people "roll," or combine, their credit card debt into their mortgage.

What Are Points?

When you obtain a mortgage you have the ability to lower your interest rate. To do this, you can purchase "points." Think of points as a form of prepaid interest. One point equals 1% of your overall loan amount. If you choose to pay points, you'll be able to get a lower rate than had you not paid points.

If you're thinking about buying points, you should consider the number of years before you sell your home or pay off your loan by refinancing. As the number of years you own your home increases, the money you spent to buy points is spread out over more years giving you time to recoup those costs. If you're planning to stay in your home for a long time, it might make sense for you to buy points. On the other hand, if you intend to be in your home for only a few years, buying points may not be in your best interest.

Your Credit Matters

Your credit history is an important element mortgage lenders consider when deciding whether or not to grant you a loan. While it's certainly not the only factor lenders take into account, it is very important.

Credit bureaus and credit reporting agencies are in the business of gathering, maintaining and selling information about people's credit histories. Bureaus and agencies collect information about your payment habits from entities such as banks, finance companies and retailers and sell this information to creditors in the form of credit reports. Most information, whether positive or negative, remains on your credit report for seven years and then cycles off automatically.

Your credit report contains a credit risk score, which is an assessment of your credit-worthiness. Credit bureaus provide risk scores to lenders who use them to objectively evaluate an applicant's credit-worthiness. Although these agencies provide credit reports to mortgage lenders when people apply for loans, they do not make lending decisions. Your lender will evaluate your credit report and any other factors it considers important.

Before applying for a mortgage, get a copy of your credit report and review it for errors and discrepancies. Bills that have been paid could remain on your credit report and might cause your lender to deny the loan. Read the report carefully. If you find any inaccuracies, contact each of the three major credit bureaus—Trans Union, Experian and Equifax—to have them cleared from your report.

Types of Mortgages

Many people believe the only mortgage program that exists is the 30-year fixed-rate mortgage. Years ago this may have been true, but not anymore. Today there are hundreds of different programs to choose from, but don't let that overwhelm you. Most loans are variations of a fixed-rate mortgage, an adjustable-rate mortgage or a home equity loan. Therefore, knowledge of how these three mortgage programs work will help you to understand the majority of available loan options.

Fixed-Rate Mortgages

Fixed-rate mortgages have a fixed interest rate over the entire term of the loan and are very popular. Many people like this type of loan because it offers certainty: The interest rate never changes. And, many home buyers believe that a fixed-rate loan is the best way for them to pay off their mortgage.

If you're planning to stay in the same home for a very long time, then a fixed-rate program might be the right mortgage for you. It may also be a good option if you're likely to squander the extra money you'd have access to if you chose a different program with a lower monthly mortgage payment. If you have a hard time saving extra money, think of a fixed-rate mortgage as "forced savings."

Adjustable-Rate Mortgages (ARMs)

Adjustable-rate mortgages, or ARMs, are mortgage programs that are fixed for an introductory period (typically one, three, five or seven years), but after the fixed period, the rate adjusts based on a pre-determined index. If the index goes up, so does your interest rate and mortgage payment. Conversely, a drop in the index will reduce your rate and payment.

Perhaps the greatest benefit to an ARM is that this type of program usually offers consumers lower initial rates (and therefore, a lower initial monthly mortgage payment) than a comparable fixed-rated mortgage. For example, on a one-, three-, five- or seven- year ARM, your monthly mortgage payment for the introductory period could be significantly lower than it would be on a 15- or 30-year fixed-rate program.

People who choose an ARM will have extra money available to them. Because of the way repayment of a mortgage is calculated, ARMs also will help you build equity faster than you would with a fixed-rate loan. (Equity is the difference between the fair market value of your property and the amount you still owe on your mortgage). The reason this happens is that the initial interest rate is lower on an ARM, so more money is applied toward the principal on your loan, rather than the interest.

Additional benefits of an ARM are:

- ✓ that your interest rate could adjust downward, reducing your monthly mortgage payment
- ✓ after the fixed-rate period expires, you can refinance to another short-term fixed-rate program

Perhaps the greatest benefit for home buyers who choose an ARM, however, is that they have the ability to expedite repayment of their loans. By paying more than the required principal and interest payment each month, they can decrease the term of their loans by months or years. Consumers who have a fixed-rate mortgage also can make larger payments and pay off their loan faster, but this strategy works better with an ARM because there is less interest.

Interest-Only ARMs

Many lenders offer a variety of adjustable-rate mortgages. One of the most popular and flexible is an "interest-only" loan. With this type of mortgage, you are required to pay only the interest on your loan for a one-, three-, five-, or seven-year period of time. After that initial term, you will be required to make a payment that accounts for both the principal and interest on your loan.

Because interest-only loans are a type of adjustable-rate mortgage, they carry a lower interest rate than fixed-rate mortgages. This means that for the first few years (the initial term) you'll have a lower monthly payment than you would with a fixed-rate mortgage and therefore, extra money on hand. You can use that money to pay down the principal balance on your loan or pay off high interest debt—the choice is yours.

Assumable Mortgages

An assumable mortgage is an agreement allowing the buyer of the home to assume the payment of an existing mortgage from the seller. This could be attractive for the buyer if the interest rate on the assumable mortgage is lower than the current market rate. In addition, there are few closing costs.

If you decide to assume a loan, remember that sellers with low-rate mortgages are offering something of significant value. That means they'll likely charge more for their houses and you'll have to come up with more cash to cover the difference between the asking price and the loan balance. At the same time, if interest rates continue to climb, that assumability feature could increase in value, giving you the chance to cash out later.

Few lenders today allow mortgages to be assumed, with the exception of Federal Housing Authority and VA loans, so read all contracts carefully. Look for a "due-on-sale" clause, which means that the mortgage may not be assumable and that the seller must pay off any outstanding balance; in that case, the buyer must apply for an entirely new mortgage. Finally, it's important to remember that lenders perform the same credit, income and debt checks for an assumable loan as they do for a conventional loan.

Federal Housing Authority (FHA) Loans

The Government does what it can to encourage home ownership through tax benefits and loan programs. A Federal Housing Authority loan is often called the "first-time buyer's mortgage." FHA loans require a much smaller down payment than conventional loans, often less than 5%.

FHA loans, while ideal for first-time buyers, are available to everyone regardless of their income level or how many homes they've owned in the past. FHA loans are also a good choice for people who have had credit problems or bankruptcies that would exclude them from obtaining a loan through conventional channels. The government focuses on the current debt-to-income ratios of FHA loan applicants, not their credit history—an advantage for many prospective buyers!

The only restriction on FHA loans is the amount of money you can borrow. Although the limits vary by county and state, they are frequently out of step with the cost of real estate in hot markets and high-priced areas. In spite of these limits, the benefits of FHA loans are clear: If you are short on cash for a down payment or have less than ideal credit and live in an area in which FHA loan caps are in sync with housing prices, you may want to take advantage of the FHA program.

 To see current FHA loan limits, check out https://entp.hud.gov/idapp/html/hicostlook.cfm

What Mortgage Program Should I Choose?

When selecting a mortgage, it's important to choose a program that best fits your particular circumstances. Unfortunately, there isn't one program that is best for everyone.

If you expect to be in the same home for 30 years and are completely risk averse, then a long-term fixed-rate program is probably a good choice. However, if you want to pay off high-interest credit card debt, pay down student loans or invest some money in your 401(k) program, then a fixed-rate option might not be the best program for you. An adjustable-rate mortgage may be a better choice because it has a lower starting interest rate than a fixed-rate mortgage, which would result in a lower monthly mortgage payment and extra cash to pay down debt or invest.

Since the majority of Americans move every five to seven years, fixed-rate programs aren't appropriate for most people. You should weigh the pros and cons of choosing a fixed-rate mortgage and an adjustable-rate mortgage by working with a professional or using one of the online calculators available on many lenders' websites. Use the Mortgage Shopping Worksheet at the end of this chapter to help you compare your options.

Lock-Ins: A lock-in, also called a rate-lock or rate commitment, is a lender's promise to hold a certain interest rate and a number of points for you, usually for a specified period of time, while your loan application is processed.

Pro: Lock-Ins protect you against increases while your application is processed.
Con: You may not be able to take advantage of price decreases during this period.

Private Mortgage Insurance (PMI)

If your down payment is less than 20% of the purchase price of your home, many lenders require you to pay private mortgage insurance (otherwise known as PMI). PMI covers your lender's loss if you default and continues until the principal on your loan is less than 80% of the property's value. At that point, lenders stop charging PMI, subject to certain conditions.

Many lenders have special mortgage programs to help you avoid paying PMI even if you're unable to make a 20% down payment. These types of loans are a great option because they offer potential tax benefits; PMI isn't tax-deductible, while the interest you pay each month on your mortgage may be (consult your tax advisor for specific details). A slightly higher interest rate is charged for these types of loans, but a PMI premium can be avoided.

For FHA loans, the government requires that you pay mortgage insurance known as a "mortgage insurance premium." Mortgage insurance on an FHA loan is due throughout the life of the loan; the only way to avoid it is to refinance out of your loan and into another mortgage program.

Home Equity Loans

Once you've been in your home for a while and have made steady mortgage payments, you will begin to accrue *equity*. As a homeowner, you can turn that equity into cash you can use. A home equity loan is generally a second mortgage secured by the equity you've acquired in your home. The term of a home equity loan can range from five to 30 years.

Home Equity Line of Credit (HELOC)

A home equity line of credit, often referred to as a HELOC, can be very useful. It is similar to a credit card except that it uses the equity in your home as the revolving line of credit. You only pay interest when you access your credit line. Unlike credit cards, the interest on a HELOC is usually tax-deductible (consult your tax advisor for more information).

A HELOC is a good choice if you'd like ready access to your equity. Many people use this type of loan to cover the cost of a home improvement project. Others find that setting up a HELOC is a great way to prepare for an unexpected, but costly, emergency.

Other advantages of HELOCs include:

✓ They are easy to tap into

✓ Monthly statements show your balance and minimum payment

✓ You can tailor your payment to meet your needs by paying off the entire balance or making minimum monthly payments.

The following three examples further illustrate the advantages of a HELOC:

EXAMPLES

➲ **Coping with a Credit Crunch:** Paul and Karen are in a short-term financial crunch. They're having difficulty paying their monthly bills, including credit card and student loan payments. By consolidating debt and using the money from a HELOC, they are able to make their minimum monthly payments.

➲ **Minimizing Monthly Payments:** With their son starting college, Mark and April use a HELOC to manage large tuition payments. They draw tuition fees each quarter and only pay the minimum on what they've drawn. By tapping their equity in smaller amounts each quarter, they pay less interest than if they had borrowed all the money at the beginning of the process.

➲ **Home Improvement Projects:** Jim wants to remodel his bathroom, but doesn't want to pay for the project by racking up high-interest credit card debt. By using a HELOC, Jim is able to avoid a high-interest rate plus the interest he pays might be tax-deductible.

When Should I Apply for a Mortgage?

Apply for a loan before you even begin searching for that new house. Some lenders will allow you to get pre-qualified while others will help you get pre-approved. It's important that you understand the difference.

Pre-qualification is an informal discussion between a borrower and lender about how much the borrower can afford. The lender doesn't verify anything, relying completely on what the borrower says about his credit history, assets, debts, income, etc. Unlike loan pre-approval, pre-qualification is not a guarantee that a borrower can secure a loan. Pre-approval is a lengthier, formal process that includes checking the borrower's credit history in addition to verifying assets, employment, income, liabilities and available cash reserves.

A pre-approval letter from a reputable lender carries more weight than a pre-qualification letter because it is assurance that your financing and offer are secure. For that reason, many sellers will accept an offer from someone who has been pre-approved for a home loan over someone who has been pre-qualified, even if his offer is lower.

Applying early for a loan has additional benefits:

✓ You know exactly how much you can afford

✓ You're in a better position to negotiate a lower price because the seller knows your offer is good

✓ You can close on a home in a matter of days—not weeks—potentially saving the seller a lot of money, which is another bargaining chip

✓ You're a virtual cash buyer—it's like shopping for a home with the money in your pocket

Do Your Research

Before you start house hunting, do some research. The Internet is a wonderful resource for countless informative articles that explain the mortgage process in great detail. In fact, many lenders have online mortgage calculators that will answer a variety of tough questions, including:

• How much money can I borrow?

• What is my price range?

• What are the tax savings associated with home ownership?

Simplifying the Process

Once upon a time when home buyers applied for home loans, they had to take time off work to meet their lenders, fill out reams of paperwork, wait days to find out if they'd been approved for a loan and then wait weeks to close. Not anymore! Many lenders now have online tools that allow you to apply for a loan from the comfort of your own home. With new and innovative technology, you even can sign your mortgage documents electronically.

How Do I Find a Reputable Mortgage Banker?

Whether you decide to work with a mortgage banker, credit union or another lending entity, it is crucial to choose a reputable, experienced mortgage professional who is associated with a company that isn't likely to go out of business when rates increase. Since there are thousands of mortgage companies in the United States, selecting a mortgage expert can be challenging. Seek out recommendations from relatives and friends.

What is "Closing?"

You've found a home and a mortgage too, but there's one more step before you move in and start making mortgage payments. "Closing" completes your real estate sale and loan transaction. Some, or all, of the following parties can attend a closing: seller, buyer, lender, the seller's mortgage holder, attorneys and the title company representative.

At the closing you will sign a variety of documents that make your home purchase official. You will also be responsible for paying several different fees, such as title insurance, private mortgage insurance, legal fees and property taxes, to name a few. Closing costs vary by state, but generally will total several thousand dollars.

The timing of your closing is very important and depending on the date, can save you quite a bit of money. For example, if you're currently renting an apartment, you'll want to schedule your closing toward the end of your lease to avoid paying unnecessary rent.

For more on the closing process, see "From Contract to Closing" beginning on page 61.

Ready to Buy Your Dream Home?

Today, purchasing a home is easier and more convenient than ever before. Thanks to the power of the Internet, you can apply for and close on your loan quickly and efficiently. Armed with the information in this book and the research you can do online, you're ready to go find that dream house. Happy hunting!

Mortgage Shopping Worksheet [1]

	Lender 1	Lender 2
Name of Lender:		
Name of Contact:		
Date of Contact:		
Mortgage Amount:		

BASIC INFORMATION ON THE LOANS

	mortgage 1	mortgage 2	mortgage 3	mortgage 4
Type of Mortgage: fixed-rate, adjustable-rate, conventional, FHA, other?				
Minimum down payment:				
Loan term (length of loan):				
Contract interest rate:				
Annual percentage rate:				
Points (may be called loan discount points):				
Monthly Private Mortgage Insurance (PMI) premiums:				
How long must you keep PMI?				
Estimated monthly escrow for taxes & hazard insurance:				
Estimated monthly payment (principal, interest, taxes, insurance, PMI):				

FEES
Different institutions may have different names for some fees and may charge different fees. We have listed some typical fees you may see on loan documents.

	mortgage 1	mortgage 2	mortgage 3	mortgage 4
Application fee or loan processing fee:				
Origination fee or underwriting fee:				
Lender fee or funding fee:				
Appraisal fee:				
Attorney fees:				
Document preparation and recording fees:				
Broker fees (may be quoted as points, origination fees, or interest rate add-on):				
Credit report fee:				
Other fees:				

Other Costs at Closing/Settlement

Title search/Title insurance For lender:				
For you:				
Estimated prepaid amounts for interest, taxes, hazard insurance, payments to escrow:				
State & local taxes, stamp taxes, transfer taxes:				
Flood determination:				
Prepaid Private Mortgage Insurance (PMI):				
Surveys & home inspections:				
Total Fees and Other Closing/Settlement Cost Estimates				

OTHER QUESTIONS AND CONSIDERATIONS ABOUT THE LOAN

	mortgage 1	mortgage 2	mortgage 3	mortgage 4
Are any of the fees or costs waivable?				

Prepayment Penalties:

	mortgage 1	mortgage 2	mortgage 3	mortgage 4
Is there a prepayment penalty?				
If so, how much is it?				
How long does the penalty period last?				
Are extra principal payments allowed?				

Lock-ins:

	mortgage 1	mortgage 2	mortgage 3	mortgage 4
Is the lock-in agreement in writing?				
Is there a fee to lock-in?				
When does the lock-in occur (at application, approval, or some other time)?				
How long will the lock-in last?				
If the rate drops before closing, can you lock-in at a lower rate?				

If the loan is an adjustable-rate mortgage:

What is the initial rate? _____ _____ _____ _____

What is the maximum the
rate could be next year? _____ _____ _____ _____

What are the rate and
payment caps each year
and over the life of the
loan? _____ _____ _____ _____

What is the frequency of rate
change and of any
changes to monthly
payment? _____ _____ _____ _____

What is the index the
lender will use? _____ _____ _____ _____

[1] *Source: The Federal Reserve Board; www.federalreserve.gov/pubs/mortgage/mortb_1.htm from a brochure prepared by the following agencies: Department of Housing and Urban Development, Department of Justice, Department of the Treasury, Federal Deposit Insurance Corporation, Federal Housing Finance Board, Federal Reserve Board, Federal Trade Commission, National Credit Union Administration, Office of Federal Housing Enterprise Oversight, Office of the Comptroller of the Currency, Office of Thrift Supervision*

Who are Fannie Mae, Ginnie Mae and Freddie Mac?

Despite their folksy sounding names, they're not real people. In 1938, the government created the Federal National Mortgage Authority, FNMA, or Fannie Mae. In 1968, Fannie Mae went public but retained its government charter. Fannie Mae's mission is "to tear down barriers, lower costs, and increase the opportunities for home ownership and affordable rental housing for all Americans. Because having a safe place to call home strengthens families, communities, and our nation as a whole." In short, Fannie Mae's job is to assure that money is readily available for home loans.

In fact, most of the money for mortgage loans in the U.S. comes from Fannie Mae, Ginnie Mae or Freddie Mac. These secondary market lenders provide banks and credit unions with a reliable source of money to fund mortgage loans made to consumers. Ensuring this steady flow of cash helps to keep the mortgage market healthy and loans affordable for consumers. Visit www.FannieMae.com and www.FreddieMac.com to learn more.

Finding Your Ideal Home

Brian Yui
CEO, HouseRebate.com

What Type of Home is for You?

The most common types of dwellings are single-family homes, condominiums and town houses. A single family home is typically a detached home on its own lot. The owner is responsible for all aspects of the property, including the interior, exterior and landscaping. A condominium is a real estate project in which an individual owner holds title to a particular unit in a building, undivided interest in the common areas of the property and, sometimes, the exclusive use of parts of the common areas.

Condominiums usually have a governing board called the Homeowners Association (HOA) that oversees the maintenance, rules and regulations of the development. Most condominiums have a monthly HOA fee that may cover expenses such as exterior building insurance, landscaping, pool maintenance, trash, water and a reserve for future capital improvements. The fee varies according to the project and its amenities.

Before entering into a purchase agreement to buy a condominium, a prospective buyer should review the past minutes of the board of directors to ascertain if there is a current or pending lawsuit against the project that might affect its future value. Reviewing the project budget and financial conditions to ensure that there are adequate reserves for future capital improvements is also wise. If a project is under-funded, the HOA could make a special assessment in the future requiring owners to contribute additional funds over and above their monthly dues.

Town houses are another option. Town houses are legally classified as condominiums, but usually share at least one common wall and are generally situated in rows so that there are no units above each other. Row homes are an example of town houses.

It's also possible to purchase a property that appears to be a single family home on its own lot but is part of a Planned Urban Development (PUD). Technically, this makes the home a condominium because there may be some shared ownership of common areas.

Location! Location! Location!

Once you decide upon a single family home, condominium or town home, you need to research where to live—or more realistically—where you can afford to live. Research community information at the library, on the Internet, or enlist the help of local real estate agents. Concentrate your search on those areas that seem desirable to you. Once you've narrowed the field, visit the area's Chamber of Commerce and check out city websites that include crime rates, demographics and school district ratings.

You may also want to evaluate the area's shopping and business services, entertainment, park and recreation facilities, public transportation, traffic congestion, noise levels (especially at night), pollution from nearby industry and the ambiance or general upkeep of the neighborhood. While some of these factors, such as recreation facilities or the quality of the school district may not be important to you, they could significantly impact the home's resale value.

Length of Stay

The longer you stay in a home, the better chance you have to make money on your investment. Keep in mind that when you sell a house, brokerage fees and closing costs will run from 6% to 8% of the selling price. Accordingly, if you sell your house before it appreciates 6% to 8%, you may experience a loss.

Generally, it takes at least three to four years to recoup buying and selling costs. However, if you are able to purchase your home during a buyer's market when supply exceeds demand and then find that economic conditions improve, you may see faster appreciation on your investment. Check the trends in your area to better determine the appropriate time period to recover your costs.

Planning for the Future

What features do you need in a home to satisfy your lifestyle now? What might you want or need five years from now? Depending on how long you plan to stay in your home, make sure the home has the amenities that your family requires. For example, a two-bedroom cottage may be perfect for a young couple with no children; however, before long, the couple could quickly outgrow the space. Young families should consider a home with room to grow and consider whether there is space to add on or if existing property boundaries will limit their ability to expand as needed.

Other good questions to ask include the following:

- Does the floor plan suit your family's style of living?
- How do the appliances compare to what would be optimal?
- What décor would you like to change?
- Is there ample space for more than one car?
- What are your plans for the yard?

Having an idea of your future needs will enable you to find a home that suits you for years to come.

Need vs. Want

We all have an imaginary dream home. Whether yours is a gingerbread Victorian with a picket fence or a top floor penthouse with views forever, recognizing the difference between what you want and what you can't live without makes all the difference.

Begin by making a wish list of all your "wants" including size, location and amenities. Think about the type of neighborhood you desire: Is it an urban landscape or a suburb with peaceful, tree-lined streets? Do you want an old house with bay windows and stained glass or a newly constructed home in which you may be the first occupant?

Once you've made your wish list, it's time for a reality check. Unless you're one of the few people with unlimited financial resources, you'll have to compromise here and there. Take some time to consider what you really need. Chances are, the number of bedrooms you need to accommodate you and your family is more important than the stained glass windows on your wish list.

Take your wish list of "wants" and prioritize them according to your lifestyle and your pocketbook. House hunting with your needs rather than your wants in mind guarantees that, at the end of the day, your home will meet your most important requirements.

New vs. Resale Homes

The difference between choosing a new home and an older model can significantly affect many of the costs and steps in the purchasing process. Maintaining a new home in the early years can cost considerably less than a resale home because everything is new and generally under warranty for the first year. Another advantage to new homes is that buyers usually have a say in the design and layout.

 Check out one of the many websites that feature new homes only, such as www.newhomes.com.

On the other hand, older homes available for resale may have imperfections and involve some compromise or renovation. Often, buyers will request that sellers purchase home warranty plans, providing coverage for the home's major appliances and systems; this type of protection is usually not covered under a homeowner's insurance policy. A home warranty plan that includes service from reputable repair companies is a tremendous value, providing peace of mind and savings on potentially unforeseen expenditures.

New homes, however, are not available in every area. And, unlike resale homes, new homes may not include pricey upgrades such as landscaping or window treatments, so you'll need to factor those costs into a comparison.

House Hunting Begins

There are several ways to find homes for sale in your preferred area. Driving through the neighborhoods that interest you is a good place to start. Take down the phone numbers on "For Sale" signs and call the owners or real estate agents for more information. The real estate section of the local Sunday paper is another excellent resource. There, you'll find a combination of listings, such as homes for sale directly by owners and others offered by real estate agents and brokers.

Many newspapers now have their real estate ads online. Recent surveys show that more than 74% of potential home buyers use the Internet to search for property. The Internet enables buyers to cover more ground quickly and efficiently by highlighting homes and statistics at the large real estate portals such as Realtor.com (www.realtor.com) and MSN House and Home (houseandhome.msn.com). These sites list the brokers' names and phone numbers, but generally do not provide addresses of individual homes.

Real estate agents and real estate companies have listings on their websites, but are usually limited to their company's listings only. A few companies provide all listings in a specified area, including those of other real estate brokers; they also offer the addresses of the homes. To find a local real estate agent's or company's website use the search function of Yahoo (www.yahoo.com) or Google (www.google.com), type in, for example, "Houston Real Estate" and browse through the results.

Some real estate company sites offer potential buyers automatic daily email notifications of homes coming on the market that meet specific purchasing criteria. This is a worthwhile and convenient feature that keeps buyers informed of the latest listings. Ask your agent about this service.

People who sell their homes without real estate agents are called, "For Sale by Owners," or "FSBOs" (pronounced fizz-bos). FSBOs generally account for less than 10% of the real estate that is for sale. These homes may present potential for considerable savings because the agent's commission is eliminated. You may need a lawyer or agent to navigate the buying process, but these opportunities may be worth investigating.

Setting Up Tours

Once you've compiled a list of homes you'd like to see, it's time to arrange the tours. It may be helpful to secure the services of a buyer's agent by getting recommendations from friends, co-workers and family members. Keep in mind, however, real estate agents often do not assist buyers interested in FSBOs because there is usually no commission paid by the owners to the agent (see next section). Buyers' agents, however, can be hired for a fixed or hourly fee to assist clients with FSBOs. Since sellers' agents commonly receive a commission from the seller based on the amount of the sale, they may not have the buyers' interest in mind. Finally, hiring an attorney to scrutinize contracts and provide advice on any complex negotiations is a good idea.

Discuss all your needs—type of area, style of home, amenities, etc.—with your real estate agent. Agents can assist you further by accessing a Multiple Listing Service. The Multiple Listing Service, or MLS, is a database of homes for sale within a specific area; the local real estate agents who belong to the local real estate association supply the listings.

The MLS generally provides photographs of the homes and the following details of the properties for sale:

- Price
- Amenities
- Utilities
- Annual property taxes
- Current financing
- Listing company

Together, you and your agent can select the properties you would like to see, set appointments and preview homes.

New homes are often sold directly by the developer and usually don't involve a buyer's real estate agent. The developer frequently will have its own in-house agent on site, however, a minority of developers will pay a commission to a buyer's agent. Your best bet is to stop by the project offices for information and to check out the model homes.

Real Estate Commissions

Real estate commissions generally work as follows: The seller enters an agreement with the listing agent to sell the home. The commission rates ordinarily range from 5% to 7% of the purchase price depending upon geographic location. If the commission is 6%, for example, when a home is sold, the commission is generally split equally between the listing agent and the buyer's agent. In other words, if a home sells for $300,000, the listing agent receives $9,000 (3% of $300,000) and the buyer's agent receives $9,000 (3% of $300,000). The seller pays for both commissions from the sale of the home; the buyer generally does not pay a commission.

 Don't forget: Real estate commission rates are not set by law and are negotiable!

With growing frequency, discount real estate brokers who share their commissions with buyers are being sought by savvy house hunters. These agents will share about one-third of their commission, or 1%, with the buyer. In the previous example, the buyer could obtain a rebate of $3,000 (1/3 x $9,000). In the past, a buyer might receive a gift basket, bottle of champagne or a thank you card. These new programs offered by discount brokers represent a significant savings and may be tax-free depending upon the structure of the rebate. Please note, however, that several states prohibit the rebating of commissions. Check with your local Department of Real Estate.

Be sure to choose a discount real estate company that is prepared to offer you full-service, walking you through every step of the home buying process.

One reputable and nationwide firm that offers these discounts is HouseRebate.com (www.HouseRebate.com). There may also be local brokers offering these reductions in your area. How are discount firms able to pass on the savings to consumers? Since approximately seven out of 10 home buyers take advantage of real estate listing information on the Internet, agents spend less time searching for homes for their clients. In addition, these discount brokers often provide the addresses of the homes online so buyers can drive by properties on their own. This further reduces the time agents need to spend with their clients.

With a traditional agent, buyers may feel guilty that they're wasting an agent's time when, after several excursions and planned property tours, they still haven't purchased a home. By having access to the addresses provided by the websites, however, buyers can view homes without guilt or sales pressure. Agents, in turn, are more willing to share their commissions with buyers who've done some of the research on their own. Once the buyer approves of the home's exterior, the discount agent will make an appointment to view the interior, accompany clients on tours and provide all the usual services of a traditional agent, such as checking on sales comparables, negotiating the deal, preparing the purchase contract and managing the entire transaction.

Discounting of fees has been prevalent in many other industries for years. Stock brokerage companies like Charles Schwab, for instance, have offered similar reductions to consumers who choose not to pay full commissions but still want to receive full service. Rebating commissions is a trend that will likely increase. Home buyers are turning to the Internet more and more to search for homes and seek neighborhood information.

What to Look for in a Home

When viewing a property it's important to find the answers to the following questions. For more helpful tools, check out "The Smart Buyer's Checklist" beginning on page 109.

CHECKLIST

➲ **Land & Location:**

- Does the area have, or will it have, amenities such as convenient shopping and public transportation?
- Is there excessive air traffic or highway noise?
- Is the property on or near a flood plain?
- Is the land free from dense trees, steep grading or water seepage? Consult an engineer to assess the block when considering add-ons or if landslip is a concern, check with a geo-technical engineer.
- Are the electricity and sewer connected?

The Exterior:

- Are there signs of dampness around windowsills?
- Are the walls free from major cracks?
- Is the paint in good condition?
- Are all the fences, retaining walls and walkways in good condition?
- Are the down pipes, gutters and roof in good condition?
- Is there an adequate carport or garage?
- Is space available to renovate and add on?
- Has the property already been added to? If so, have the proper permits been obtained?
- Is the pool or spa equipment in good working order?
- Does pool fencing comply with current safety standards?

The Interior:

- Is the foundation level and in good condition?
- Are ceilings, floors and walls in good condition and free of moisture and mold?
- Is the structure fully insulated?

- Are the light fixtures and window treatments included in the sales price?
- Are natural lighting and ventilation adequate throughout the home?
- Do the doors and windows open and close properly?
- Are power outlets sufficient and suitably located?
- Are doorways and halls wide enough to accommodate your furniture?
- Will your furniture complement the home?

Kitchen:

- Is there adequate cupboard, counter and storage space?
- If the home doesn't have them, is there room for a dishwasher and microwave?
- Is the exhaust system adequate?
- Are there sufficient outlets? Are they conveniently located?

Bathrooms:

- Are there exhaust fans and sufficient ventilation?
- Are showers and tubs free from leaks? Are there any cracks in the tiles?
- Are the toilets in good working order and condition?
- Are there enough electrical outlets? Is the light adequate?
- Are there cupboards, mirrors and other amenities?

Bedrooms:

- Are bedrooms near a busy intersection, bright streetlights or subject to the glare of passing vehicle headlights?
- Are lighting and ventilation adequate?
- Is there sufficient closet space?

Laundry/Service Area:

- Can your washing machine and/or dryer be installed without any problem?
- Is the size and type of hot water service suitable?
- Are there sufficient electrical outlets?

The Offer

It has likely taken several weeks of research and legwork, but you've found the home that best suits your needs. Now what? Is there a formula to plug in or rules to consult before making an offer? How much should you offer the seller? Is it really how much you offer or how you present your terms that will make or break the deal?

Before making an offer you will need to determine a reasonable market price for the desired home. Your real estate agent will run a *comparable market analysis (comp)* for you on similar homes that have sold in the same neighborhood within the past year. This will help you to assess the neighborhood's general trends. Comparing the amenities, condition and location of similar homes that have already sold and then weighing those factors alongside the current market is the first step to making a reasonable offer.

Next, decide how much you are willing to pay for the home. If you are willing to pay the market value or more because you have your heart set on a house and don't want to risk losing it, you must share this with your agent. Most reputable agents will try to negotiate a below-market sales price because they want to keep you as a client. If this is the house for you and you are prepared to overpay in order to get it, then your agent's negotiating tactics will depend heavily on this information.

Finally, try to discern what is most important to the seller. Is the seller highly motivated because he has already purchased another home? Is a relocation or divorce part of the equation? Try to find out why he is selling his home. It may give you some insight into negotiating strategy. Perhaps the seller wants to close escrow within a certain timeframe; if so, he may be willing to take less for his home if you are willing to accommodate his requests.

For expert guidance on negotiating a home purchase (or sale), check out "Winning Bidding Strategies" beginning on page 45.

Worried about getting into a bidding war? See "How to Make Offers in 'Hot Markets'" beginning on page 119.

Submitting the Offer

An offer is usually presented in a "Purchase Agreement." (Please see the sample beginning on page 140).

Unless you offer the full listing price of the property, the seller will likely submit a "Counter Offer" to you. (Please see the sample on page 148). The counter offer outlines the changes the seller wants to make to your original offer. As the buyer, you can accept the counter offer or submit another counter offer with further amendments to the seller's counter offer. This process can continue until the price and terms of both parties are mutually agreed upon—or aren't.

If and when both parties agree to the terms, the purchase contract and the counter offers (if applicable) are signed by both parties and escrow, or closing, begins.

How to Buy Property with No Money Down

Robert G. Allen
Author of "Nothing Down" & Other Best-Sellers

Your goal is to buy a house, something you can live in happily and afford easily. Great! Even if you don't have a large down payment, the creative techniques that follow may help you to locate and negotiate a better deal.

Getting Around the Cash Crunch

There are two major problems that affect numerous young people today: Many are unable to qualify for a loan (because their incomes are too low or their credit rating is poor) and others can't come up with the required down payment. These problems are real, but hardly insurmountable.

In fact, that ever-elusive creature called a mortgage can be yours even if your income is low and your credit rating is less than desirable. Your greatest asset is the knowledge that you can buy a house without involving a bank. You can buy directly from the seller, and you can have the seller carry the loan himself on a land contract, a contract of sale, or a wraparound mortgage (a prior mortgage, or money owed, by the mortgagee to a third party). There are many sellers who will agree to these terms—some to avoid tax problems, others to create a monthly cash flow during retirement—so you should be out there looking for that new house!

You may not be in a financial position to buy your dream house right now, but the home you are about to buy can be a stepping-stone to a bigger and better house somewhere down the road.

Don't let your pride get in the way. Each step you take will bring you closer to your destination. Each time you buy a smaller house, you will be building up equity for that larger ideal house. Move through several houses, possibly making several thousand dollars in profits on each move, until you are able to invest in your dream house—free and clear. It's well worth it.

Your best bet as you begin your search will be to deal with competent, trustworthy real estate agents who know all the ins and outs, and therefore, can help you in countless ways. If you have absolutely no down payment to work with, find a real estate agent who is willing to receive his commission from the sale in the form of a note. If you can't find one who is willing to do that, try to learn as much about real estate as you can and go it alone. Don't be timid about discussing and brainstorming ideas with the seller, the seller's attorney and anyone else who could have an impact on the decision to buy or sell a house. Ask probing questions; there are solutions other than cash and it's your job to find them.

If you don't have a real estate agent, you'll have to do a lot of searching yourself. Try to find a "don't wanter"—someone who will be flexible in the terms of the sale and will agree to carry a loan instead of insisting on a large cash down payment. Look for people who are managing properties from out of state; they're usually the ones who are weary of the management hassle and will agree to your terms.

Don't despair. Finding the right combination—a "don't wanter," a property that suits your needs perfectly and terms that fit your budget—takes time. Don't give up; the house you are looking for may be just around the corner. Keep searching until you find it.

If you come across a good bargain with a seller who is willing to be flexible but also insists on some cash, consider bringing in a partner. Your partner provides the cash down payment. You agree to make the mortgage payments, keep the property in top condition and even make improvements while you live there. Then, when you sell the house, you'll split any profit with your partner. Convincing a partner that his investment is safe may take some effective talking, but you'll probably be able to show him a respectable return on his investment. Do your research and use all of your knowledge of real estate to persuade your partner to help you with the cash outlay.

Creative Solutions

You might try the earnest money option: Find a property that's a good bargain, tie it up with an *earnest money deposit* to show your commitment, find another buyer immediately and resell the property for a profit. Voila! You've earned your down payment!

If you belong to a credit union, you should consider borrowing the down payment. This might mean that your payments are higher until you repay the loan, but it is better than saving for a down payment—something that may never happen! You might have to hang on by your fingernails until you get that loan paid off, but if you find the right property, your purchase will pay you many times over.

Look for properties on which the seller is delinquent two or three mortgage payments. These sellers are motivated and often flexible in their terms.

Search for a house that is up for lease; persuade the seller to give you an option to buy within a certain period of time. This technique locks in the price now and gives you the opportunity later (if you have negotiated a hard bargain) to sell the home for a price well above the option price. Again, you've just earned a down payment for the next purchase!

As a last resort, find an individual with a strong financial statement who is willing to cosign on your loan.

Special Programs

Any of the above techniques can be used to come up with the down payment. You should also be aware of special programs available to home buyers:

- The Federal Housing Authority (FHA) guarantees loans for people who don't have large down payments.

  Under FHA loans, which can be obtained through most banks and savings and loan associations, you verify that you qualify for a low-down-payment loan.

Depending upon the price of the home, you could obtain a loan with a down payment as low as 3%. The interest rate is generally lower than it is when borrowing with any other arrangement.

There are a couple of disadvantages: The loans take longer to obtain and the appraisals are usually low (something that can cause a problem at closing).

- The Veterans Administration sponsors a program for veterans. If you've served in the armed forces, you can buy a home with no down payment; however, you will have to be prepared to pay closing costs.

- Local savings and loan associations frequently make special offers to home buyers. A qualified buyer can often buy a home for as little as 5% down. Check around your area to see if any such programs are available.

- Many state and local governments are trying to solve their housing crises by offering tax-free bonds to generate funds for low-interest rate loans to low-income people.

These funds often go unclaimed because few people know about the various government programs.

Some mortgage brokers now offer 100% financing. Contact your local lenders to investigate.

Success Stories

Other creative options include:

Using Talent, Not Cash

Depending upon the seller, you may be able to trade him some of your valuable services as part of the down payment. If you are an accountant or attorney, you could give the seller credits toward the use of your services; for instance, offer to do his taxes for the next 10 years. I once offered a building contractor a partial equity in a building lot I owned in exchange for the use of his labor on my personal residence. He agreed to do all the carpentry work on my home without charge in exchange for my equity in a $14,000 building lot upon which he could build himself a home. We both came out ahead and happy.

High Monthly Down Payments

If you are blessed with a high monthly surplus cash flow but don't want to wait to save for the down payment, consider offering the seller his equity in the form of a very high monthly payment.

For example, suppose a seller wanted to sell, but he needed some cash for his $100,000 home with a $6,000 equity. Offer to buy his home with no down payment, assume his existing loan of $94,000 and make a $500 monthly payment at 12% interest on his remaining equity. An anxious seller may agree because he knows that he can get his full price this way rather than a lower price with an all-cash offer.

This technique offers you the flexibility of having at least 30 days to find another buyer if you are going to sell the property for quick profit. It also acts as a forced savings plan: At the end of 12 months you will have paid over $6,000 cash to buy the property, but the property will likely have appreciated during that period of time.

Compare the return to that of a savings account: $500 a month into a bank account plus 1% interest will grow to about $6,033 before taxes. The same $500 toward equity in a home nets you at least as much, including loan equity build-up if the property appreciates in value by only 5% ($100,000 x .05 = $5,000). You could more than double your money. The obvious winner is the real estate purchase.

Raising the Price, Lowering the Terms

If you determine that the seller is more concerned about his price than about what he receives in the form of cash, appeal to his sense of greed.

Using the numbers from the previous example, offer him a price of $105,000 if he will sell the building to you with no-down or low-down terms. Tell him he can choose $95,000 all cash, or $105,000 with no cash down.

The real estate industry operates on a universal rule: The more cash involved in the sale, the lower the price. The converse is also true: The lower the cash, the higher the price and profit to the seller. It may be to your advantage to offer a higher price for a lower down payment.

Deferring the Down Payment with No Mortgage Payments

At one of my seminars, a repeat student related the following story; it was creative enough to include as part of the arsenal of nothing down techniques.

EXAMPLE

➲ This student had located an older six-unit building, which the seller owned free and clear of any mortgages. The property was in an excellent location and priced right. There was only one problem. The seller wanted a $10,000 down payment, which my student didn't have at the time.

The student began to use his head instead of his wallet. He reasoned that the seller had no mortgage payments to make each month and that he was wealthy enough that the lack of monthly income for a short while would not be a burden to him.

So, the student proposed that the seller turn over the property to him with no down payment and no mortgage payments for six months. Interest would accrue on the mortgage for six months; at the end of this period, normal monthly payments would commence and continue for the next 25 years until paid in full.

The seller reluctantly agreed since he was able to obtain his full asking price and terms with the small exception of the six-month delay in the down payment.

As soon as the buyer took over the property, he was able to collect the rents and the security deposits and stash them in his bank account. As each month rolled around he collected the rents and let them accrue. He paid out only necessary expenses and did all of the maintenance work himself to save money.

Since he did not have a mortgage payment to make, the majority of his income went right into savings, and during the next six months he was able to save enough money to come up with almost all the required $10,000 down payment.

For example, six units renting at $275 per month gives a gross monthly income of $1,650. In six months' time, over $9,900 has been collected from rents, not counting the tenant security deposits. If he can be frugal with his expense money, the $10,000 down payment is generated from the property rents. In effect, the buyer borrowed the down payment from the seller, who let him repay it over the next 25 years!

So, quit gazing in despair at the empty columns in your savings passbook. There is a house out there just waiting for you to move in the sofa, dust off the mantel and mow the front lawn.

The principles described here are universal and they'll work for you. Study them again and a few months from now, you might be pruning your own fruit trees while your spouse drinks lemonade from your very own back porch.

Winning Bidding Strategies

Brian Yui
CEO, HouseRebate.com

Take equal parts intuition, calculated risk-taking and research, add a pinch of psychological warfare, and you have a recipe for bidding success.

Whether you're a first-time buyer or a veteran of several home purchases, making an offer can still be intimidating. You probably won't be negotiating face-to-face with the seller; he or she will communicate with you through the listing agent.

Frequently, there are "intangible" factors in play during a negotiation. While money and terms are critically important, never underestimate the role of emotions—yours and the seller's. You may be the best at what you do, but when it comes to bidding on a home, keep your ego in check. Drive a tough bargain, but be open to compromise.

Laying the Groundwork

Be friendly with the owner. If possible, try to make small talk with the seller at an open house or the property tour. Find common ground. You have a much better chance of getting your offer accepted if the seller knows and likes you. Your offer may even win out over a higher bid from an unknown bidder.

Here are some helpful hints for communicating with the seller:

1. The home is the owner's pride and joy. When touring the property never talk about remodeling or point out features you don't like. It's not uncommon for a seller to accept a lower bid from a more enthusiastic and less critical buyer.

In one example, a seller accepted an offer $10,000 under the high bid because the high bidder indicated that he planned to tear out the existing garden. The garden was very special to the seller who wanted the new owner to preserve it. Follow your mother's advice: If you can't say something nice, say nothing at all!

2. When submitting your offer, include a letter telling the seller how much you like the house. Personalize your offer and include a brief background and picture of yourself and your family. Compliment the seller as much as possible.

3. A buyer's agent can't talk to a seller directly. Consider asking the seller questions your agent can't ask, such as why are you selling, what price are you looking for, would you consider an offer of _____? Find out what the seller's hot buttons are; for example, if the seller is concerned about finding a replacement property, offer to rent back the property for 30 to 60 days so the seller can find a new home.

4. Have your agent talk to the seller's agent to find out if there are other bids and what the seller's bottom-line price might be. Listing or seller's agents are usually prohibited from disclosing these details, however sellers will sometimes give the agent permission to share this information.

The more information you have, the better you can structure your bid. If there are no other potential offers, you could consider starting with a lower bid. In a multiple bid situation, you should submit a stronger offer at the onset, as many sellers only counter the top bidders.

How Much Should You Bid?

Find out what comparable properties are selling for. Is the trend going higher or lower? Before you enter the fray, set a limit on how much you will pay for a home. Don't get caught in a bidding frenzy that you have to win and don't overpay for a home. There will usually be another home out there for you.

1. If comparable properties are much lower than the seller's asking price, have your agent include this documentation with your offer. In rapidly rising markets, consider bidding slightly above the asking price. Your property may even go up in value during escrow.

2. If you are not emotionally attached to the property, start low and work your way up. However, consider the seller's feelings and be sure to make a reasonable offer. Starting off too low may alienate or insult the seller.

3. Have your agent put out feelers to the other agent. The listing agent may say the owner turned down an offer of $_____ already. This information gives you some insight on where to begin.

If you're bidding on:		Then:
A hot property in a hot market	➲	Offer the highest bid you can afford based on market value
A fairly priced home in a steady market	➲	Offer the asking price or just below
Property that has been on the market longer than average or overpriced property in a sluggish market	➲	Open with a low bid and slowly move up in small increments

Dealing with sellers with an "I love to negotiate" personality: If you are reaching your dollar limit in the bidding process, have your agent tell the other party that this is your final offer and that there are several other properties you are considering. If the seller says he will wait for a higher price, have your agent emphasize that you may not be around when the seller reconsiders.

Working with Value Ranges

In some areas of the country, homes are listed for sale at a range between two prices as opposed to a fixed price. This is called *value range pricing*.

For example, a home could be listed at a range of $285,000 to $315,000 versus a fixed $300,000. This value range method is a pricing strategy by the seller to capture the most potential buyers.

Prior to making an offer, have your agent determine the fair market value of the property by using sales comparables. As with all offers, you should base your bid on market value and not the value range.

Assuming the fair market value is within the seller's stated value range, bidding at the low end or below the range is a good starting point when there are no other offers. Remember that the seller is not required to accept a bid in the range; rather, he or she is stating that they will entertain offers in that range.

If you can't bear to lose the property, consider starting your bid higher than the minimum, assuming that the sales comparables justify it. In some instances, you may even consider bidding above the value range if there's competition and if market conditions warrant. Just consider your risk tolerance when you're bidding.

 Remember that the value range is just a guide. Your bidding should be based upon fair market value, your financial circumstances and your desire to own the home.

Timing Counts

If you like a property, write the offer as soon as possible. Many rookie buyers are tentative and try to do all their homework prior to making an offer, by which time the home could be sold to someone else. Remember that most contracts allow the buyer some time to check out the property, make inspections and review reports. This is called the *due diligence* period. You can usually back out of the deal during the due diligence period without a penalty, so write offers now and investigate later.

Familiarize yourself with the contracts used in your area so when the time comes, you'll be ready. Submit your offer early to get control of the property. You don't want to be the person who is most prepared for a race but starts a few days later than the competition.

Did you come in second with your offer? Ask your agent to see whether your offer can be in a backup position. If the original offer is not consummated for any reason, such as the buyer not qualifying for a loan, the property will automatically go to you. You might be surprised how many properties have been purchased by the buyer in the backup position. Be sure to have the agent include a provision in your backup offer allowing you to cancel it at anytime.

Beating the Competition

If there are competing offers, these factors may put you at the front of the home buying pack.

1. Have a short escrow and an all-cash bid. Offer to purchase the property in 21 days vs. 30 or 60 days. Make sure your lender can accommodate your terms prior to using this technique.

2. Include proof of your ability to make the down payment such as bank statements, and a loan pre-approval letter from your lender with your offer. These show the seller that you are not only serious, but also able to consummate the deal. This may give you an edge over a higher offer without similar documentation.

3. Show a bigger deposit with your offer (more than 3% of the purchase price). Higher deposits show a buyer's commitment to the home.

4. Minimize the number of contingencies in your offer.

5. If you need to sell your current home to buy your next one, then sell it first! Offers that are contingent upon the buyers selling their home first are given the least amount of consideration.

6. If you have competition, don't point out all the problems with the property in an effort to get a lower price. Instead, get the seller to accept the offer and then order a professional property inspection. Once the offer is accepted, the balance of power is tipped in your favor. Make your request for repairs toward the end of your due diligence period because the seller will be more vested in the deal at that point.

7. If you anticipate the seller taking the highest offer without negotiation, bid an odd number. If the list price is $400,000, bid $400,100. Sometimes, you'll beat the competition by a mere $100.

8. If there are multiple bids and you know some of the neighbors, ask them to put in a good word for you with the seller.

9. If you're in the counter offer phase and there are other offers, consider adding an escalation clause. You could, for example, stipulate that if there is another offer higher than yours, you will increase your bid to $2,000 over the highest offer with proof of the higher offer.

10. If you receive and approve the seller's counter offer, have your agent hand-deliver the contract to the listing agent or seller. Remember that until the seller or authorized agent confirms receipt of the accepted counter offer, or you have proof of delivery, there is no deal. Notify your agent when the acceptance is on the way, so he or she can get a head start on confirmation from the seller.

Breaking a Deadlock

Sometimes, even when everyone involved has the best intentions, the process can come to a screeching halt. Both buyer and seller may be exhausted by the negotiations or may have reached their bottom-line positions.

If this happens to you and you're still emotionally invested in making the home your own, try some of the following techniques:

1. Every good salesperson will tell you that getting to "yes" is a critical factor in achieving success. Focus on issues that you and the seller can agree upon to get the seller in the habit of saying "yes!"

2. Give up something less important to gain momentum. Consider giving in to one of the seller's demands or making a concession you can live with to achieve a lower price. Sometimes you have to give a little to get a little.

3. Propose that you and the seller split the different between your offer and the asking price.

4. Give the seller some options. Consider writing an *either/or contract*. For example, offer the seller a higher price with a longer escrow or a lower price with a shorter escrow.

5. Use the *take away clause* technique. Assume that, after several counter offers, your last bid was $290,000 and the seller's last offer was $315,000. Your personal limit is $300,000. Make a counter offer at $295,000 and give the seller two days to accept it. Let the seller know that you will pay $300,000 if he or she accepts the offer within 24 hours. This method puts pressure on the seller to respond quickly to get the extra $5,000. Some people just can't pass up a deal!

6. Know "when to hold 'em and when to fold 'em." Set a deadline for action. That way, both you and the seller can move on if there's no resolution.

 For more on bidding, see "How to Make Offers in 'Hot Markets'" beginning on page 119.

The Art of Giving In

If you absolutely, positively must have a home you've seen, you may have to meet the seller's terms and price. Remember that, sometimes, sellers are stuck on a price. They've arrived at a number and just won't budge.

If the seller wants $350,000 for his house and you are willing to pay $345,000, consider offering $350,000 and asking the seller to pay $5,000 of your closing costs. Psychologically, the seller is thinking he will receive $350,000 for his home, something he can tell his neighbors. In reality, the seller is getting $345,000 ($350,000 less $5,000 in credits).

Based on the above example, if the seller won't compromise, consider paying the extra $5,000 yourself. Five thousand dollars in the course of a 30-year mortgage may amount to only a couple extra dollars per day. Is it worth cutting out one designer coffee a day to live in this home? Ask yourself how you would feel if another buyer came in and offered the seller's magic number.

Other alternatives include accepting the seller's price, but asking him to include some furniture or appliances with the property. Or, if you want the house and just can't afford the difference in price, consider asking the seller to lend you the difference. Create a realistic repayment schedule and begin servicing the loan as soon as you are able.

What to Expect from Your Home Inspection

Keith S. Fimian
Chairman & Founder, U.S. Inspect, LLC

The home inspection is one of the many steps involved in buying a house. This chapter addresses what home buyers should expect from a professional home inspection.

The Basics

Upon arriving, a qualified inspector makes general introductions and describes what is going to take place. This is a critical part of the process because a good home inspector will want all the participants to fully understand what the assessment will cover. The inspector then explains the inspection agreement and gives the client an opportunity to review and sign it.

Next, the inspector takes the client on a detailed walk-through inspection of the home. This involves examining all visible areas and reviewing all accessible items while discussing each component or system.

Finally, the inspector completes a hard copy report for the client and, if necessary, for the agent. Some inspectors now make the report available online. The whole procedure usually takes two to three hours, depending on the age and size of the house.

A Step-by-Step Look

A home inspection consists of 10 points that are well document-ed in the Standards of Practice of the National Association of Home Inspectors. Quality home inspectors will adhere to, or even exceed, these standards:

Visual

The nature of a home inspection is visual, meaning that a visual examination of the accessible and available components of the house and permanently installed appliances will be conducted.

The visual aspect of a home inspection can be compared to a medical examination. The inspector is like a doctor who looks for observable indications of problems. Most of the time, the doctor can give a diagnosis of, or judgment about, the patient's health immediately, but sometimes he must order additional tests or refer a specialist to determine specific problems or recommend treatments. Similarly, a home inspector is professionally trained to give an immediate assessment about the home's "health" based on all the visual indicators; however, there are occasional circumstances in which the inspector will recommend that a specialist, such as a heating contractor or structural engineer, looks at a particular problem.

Since the home inspection is a visual examination of the accessible components of the house, an inspector can examine only what he sees. Items that are hidden from view, such as plumbing inside the walls, are not directly inspected, but are tested for functionality by running the faucets and so forth.

Informative Walking Consultation

A first-rate home inspector will do more than merely inspect each visual item. The purchase of a home is one of the largest investments most people ever make and buyers should be as informed and educated as possible. The home inspector can provide that education. The inspection is not only an evaluation of the home, but also an informative experience for buyers, one that teaches them about the home's systems and how they operate.

The buyers will learn the locations of the main electrical, water and gas shut-offs so they know how to turn off these utilities in the event of an emergency. The inspector also identifies the locations of all homeowner controls and instructs buyers how to work each component. For example, he'll demonstrate how the thermostat activates the furnace and air conditioner, how the garage door opener functions, etc.

It's important and reassuring to buyers when they are able to establish a positive rapport with the inspector. Professional inspectors strongly encourage the buyers to be present during the entire inspection because buyers can benefit greatly from their knowledge and experience. A good home inspection should be much more than just a report.

Operational Check of Components and Appliances

Not only does the inspector show clients how to operate controls of the home's systems, but he also tests the operability of the systems using those same homeowner controls. By the time the inspection is complete, all permanent appliances in the house will be tested to make sure they are working properly.

Inspectors do not dismantle appliances, but they do open them to look inside whenever they have homeowner access panels. On a furnace, for example, there is always an access panel provided in order to change the filter and inspectors will examine the inside of the furnace to the extent that they can see through this panel.

The one component that responsible inspectors do scrutinize more closely, which a homeowner normally would not, is the electrical panel. The frequency of electrical problems warrants that the panel cover be removed. Quality home inspectors are trained to do this properly and safely.

Representative Sampling

In many inspection agreements it is stated that the home inspection is a representative sampling of *like components*. For instance, only a representative sampling may be taken of like components such as outlets, windows and doors, which comply with the standards of the most reputable home inspection organizations.

Whenever possible, the best inspectors strive to check all like components, but sometimes they are not able to get to every outlet and window. In some cases, an inspector may be unable to access a particular room because of a sleeping baby or penned-in animals. Or, perhaps an inspector cannot view all the outlets because a large sofa is obscuring them and he is not required to move heavy furniture.

Single Point in Time

The home inspection is a report of the home's condition on a certain date or single point in time. This means that the inspector is looking at a "snapshot" of the house and reporting what he saw, how things worked and the condition of the home's systems on that particular day. For example, if the roof leaks a year later, unless there is apparent evidence of a developing problem, the inspector is not expected to foresee future problems. Inspectors do, however, look for and note such indicators as water stains, mold or mildew, which might indicate a current or surfacing problem.

A good inspection company will stand behind its work, but buyers should expect that the condition of a home would change over time.

A Home Inspection is Different from a Code Inspection

A home inspector provides an introduction to the house and an informative, educational consultation. A code inspector, on the other hand, works for the local municipality and enforces the local and state codes with little or no concern for the buyer's understanding of what the codes mean or how they apply.

Why does the buyer's home inspection exclude information about codes? The function of the home inspection is to evaluate the condition of the property, not to determine whether it conforms to code.

Furthermore, there are volumes of information contained within the building, electrical, mechanical and fire codes, and while many inspectors know a great deal about codes, it is virtually impossible for inspectors to master and keep current with all of them. Most codes change every three years; though a house built 50 or 60 years ago may have been acceptable based on the codes that were in force at that time, it may be completely out of step with today's standards (even though new codes are not applicable to old houses in most jurisdictions).

A Home Inspection is Different from an Appraisal

An appraiser looks at the house and uses specific criteria to help determine its value whereas an inspector looks at the house only to determine its condition and the condition of all its systems. The general condition of the house may be of some importance to the appraiser but only as it relates to value.

Appraisers do not climb on the roof, enter a crawlspace, or even operate the furnace or other appliances. Appraisers consider not only an overview of the condition of the house, but also its location, its proximity to desirable schools and other public facilities, its square footage, lot size and recent sales prices of comparable properties. The appraiser then formulates an opinion of the property's value for the lender.

Informed Opinion

The inspection represents the informed opinion of the professional home inspector. The home inspectors are trained to have considerable knowledge about all the systems in the home, but may not have exhaustive technical knowledge of all the details in each system. They are trained to look for certain indicators of present or future problems and offer a reasonably dependable opinion based on their knowledge and expertise.

Occasionally, an inspector discovers a problem, but the determination of its cause may go beyond the scope of the inspection. For example, certain conditions, such as excessive rust found in an old furnace, may require that a component be dismantled and investigated more exhaustively. In this case, a technical specialist, such as a heating contractor, may be needed to determine the extent of the problem and best course of action for repair. Most responsible inspectors, however, will have enough knowledge to keep such further evaluation recommendations to a minimum.

The Report is the Property of the Client

The results of an inspection are the property of the client or person who pays the inspector, typically the buyer. The inspector does not have the right to discuss inspection results with real estate agents, sellers or other interested parties without the client's permission.

In addition to confidentiality, the inspector has other obligations to his clients. A good inspector will be available for phone consultations after the inspection; however, when the client pays the inspector and signs the inspection agreement, the relationship is governed by the terms of that agreement. Moreover, the inspector's obligations remain only to the client, even if the client sells or gives away the inspection report to the seller, another buyer or any other party.

Impartiality

In the real estate industry there is a phenomenon called "buyer's remorse" whereby the buyer will use the home inspection in an attempt to get out of the contract though there may be no significant problems with the house.

The goal of a professional home inspector is to provide objective information to the client about the home. While the client may use the inspection report as a negotiating tool, the inspector does not become involved in the contractual arrangements between the buyers, sellers and real estate agents. Though the inspector is available after the inspection to answer questions and provide clarifications, the goal of an honest home inspector is to provide the most accurate information possible about a home, without exaggeration or omission.

Buyer Beware: Mold

Molds are simple, microscopic organisms in the ecosystem that break down organic materials. They can be found wherever there are organic materials and moisture, both of which are necessary for mold growth. Molds are found both indoors and outdoors in any area of the country; some are visible, some not.

Mold presents a growing real estate concern due to the potential health risk and subsequent liability that mold-contaminated homes may pose. The American Lung Association and the U.S. Consumer Product Safety Commission estimate that up to 50% of all structures have damp conditions that may encourage the development of molds and bacteria. These molds and bacteria could lead to allergic reaction, asthma and spread infection.

Though mold has been around for thousands of years, it is a relatively new worry in residential housing. Mold contamination has instigated numerous lawsuits across the country, and has headlined popular media such as Dateline NBC, Newsweek, Time and The Wall Street Journal. Sometimes referred to as "the asbestos of the new millennium," mold can result from moisture caused by roof leaks, hidden plumbing leaks and basement water penetrations.

Because the issue of mold has entered the mainstream so rapidly, science has yet to catch up. Guidelines for mold measurement and exposure have not been established yet, but

one thing is clear: As the dramatic financial toll of mold continues to rise, measures need to be implemented in order to minimize financial risk and liability exposure.

Testing and Sampling Methodologies

Although there are no defined standards or exposure limits, it
is possible to identify houses with mold contamination by
comparing the indoor and outdoor levels of mold spores using
the air sampling method. A review of the recommendations by
the nation's leading testing laboratories shows air sampling to be
the method of choice for residential mold screening.

When properties are found to have higher levels of mold indoors
than outdoors, further investigation is recommended. It is assumed
that a higher ratio of indoor mold is indicative of an internal mold
growth, which needs to be corrected. It is generally understood
that elevated levels of mold indicate some form of moisture
penetration such as a leaky roof, hidden plumbing leak or other
water infiltration problem.

Mold: The Home Inspector's Role

A home inspector's role in the process of surveying for mold problems is for
screening purposes only. Although the home may show symptoms of mold
exposure and mold may appear to be present, it is not the responsibility of the
inspector to determine its effects on the health of any particular occupant;
that would be the responsibility of a physician or industrial hygienist. It is
recommended that home buyers hire a mold specialist if they suspect any mold on
the property.

From Contract to Closing

Stewart Morris, Jr.
President & CEO, Stewart Title Company

Once you've found the home of your dreams and made an offer that the seller has accepted, you'll begin the legal process of "closing" or making the home yours.

What Does "Closing" Mean?

Closing a real estate transaction is the investigation made by a title attorney or agent to determine the following:

- All deeds, mortgage papers and other title documents necessary for the completion of the transaction have been properly executed and delivered

- All real estate taxes have been paid

- All current real estate taxes have been prorated properly between the buyer and seller

- Financial consideration (payment) has cleared and all monetary proceeds have been properly disbursed

- A final search of title has been made

- All papers of record have been filed at the courthouse

While all of this may sound daunting, in most sales, professionals such as a title agent, attorney and escrow company, as well as your real estate agent will guide you through the process.

The Basic Steps

There are several steps when transferring a land title from one owner to another. While the parties handling the steps may vary depending upon where the real estate is located, the same process applies throughout the United States. The following is an overview of how a typical real estate closing works.

Opening the title order

Upon execution of an *escrow, sales contract,* or *earnest money contract*, the closing begins. Once the title agent or attorney receives a properly completed contract a title search and examination begins.

Most of the time, an *earnest money deposit* made by the potential home buyer to show that he or she is serious about buying the house accompanies the contract. This is immediately deposited into the title agent or attorney's escrow account. Earnest money must be in the form of cash, wire transfer or check. The parties should receive a receipt that shows acceptance of both the contract and the earnest money deposit when they've been processed by the title agent or attorney. A *guaranty file* (GF) or order number is issued to the file for identification.

At this point in the closing process, it's very important that the title agent or attorney obtains a good legal description of the property to be transferred. Because title to real estate is searched by its legal description, having an incorrect description will slow down the process. Property that has been subdivided will be known by its lot and block numbers (i.e., Lot 1, Block 1, Mayfair Subdivision, Chico County, CA), while property that is still acreage in nature will be known by a metes and bounds description (i.e., Beginning at the SW intersection of Post Lane and Hwy. 21; Thence So. 650 ft. along and adjacent to...).

Processing the file

After opening the title order, the escrow or closing officer will order the tax information on the property. Prorated taxes sometimes cause confusion because most real estate taxes are paid in arrears.

Here is an example to help explain the tax payment entries that **EXAMPLE** are found on a typical closing statement:

➲ Assume that a title agent or attorney has a transaction closing on March 1 in a county where taxes are assessed annually. The seller's responsibility is the property tax amount from Jan. 1 to March 1 because the seller owned the property during this period. The buyer's responsibility for annual taxes begins on March 1. Since no one can go down to the tax office and pay a portion of the taxes for a given year, title agents or attorneys must prorate the taxes. The taxes for the part of the year that the seller has owned the property are calculated. The seller's portion of the taxes shows as an expense (charge) on the seller's side of the statement and a credit on the buyer's side of the statement.

The title agent will receive a tax certificate, tax statement or tax information that shows no past taxes are past due, or that taxes are due and payable. The title agent can collect the proper amount at closing and send that amount directly to the appropriate taxing authority.

Understanding Real Estate Taxes: Real estate or ad valorem taxes (charged according to the property's value) accrue on an annual, semiannual or quarterly basis depending on the state in which the property is located. Most real estate property taxes are "paid in arrears," which means the buyer is assessed the taxes though they aren't due and payable until a future date. The seller is responsible for all past due property taxes, including interest and penalties; these amounts will be paid prior to the transfer of property. Additionally, the seller is responsible for a prorated portion of the property taxes from the assessment to the closing date, so the buyer will be credited the amount of taxes that the seller owes at the close of escrow. At that time, the buyer pays the entire tax bill, which is partially covered by the credit from the seller.

The title agent or attorney will then verify that the legal description, address, owner's name and the exemptions filed for the property match the county tax rolls. Correct tax information is crucial to make the correct tax proration when closing documents are prepared.

If the property is a lot and block property—for instance, a home on a subdivision lot—that existed for quite a while, there are relatively few problems that can arise. Rural acreage, however, can present challenges related to agricultural or open space land exemptions. If the property you're purchasing is rural in nature, those special use exemptions may entail investigation and work to be done before the title agent will be able to guarantee taxes paid through a certain date or year.

The seller's loan payoff amount and cost per day of the loan, known as "per diem cost," is usually ordered next. Title agents and attorneys are required by their title underwriters to have pay-off information in writing. If the buyer is assuming the seller's loan then the assumption documentation should be in writing as well. The seller should supply the account or loan number and the name in which the account is carried to the title agent or attorney as soon as possible.

Homeowner and maintenance fees are then requested from the appropriate parties. Most condominiums and residential properties located in an urban area are subject to some sort of maintenance fee that is collected for the upkeep of the common areas. Title agents and attorneys will confirm that the dues are current, whether there is a reserve account to be transferred to the buyer, and if there are requirements by the HOA connected with the transfer of the account. Some associations require a copy of the contract or a letter stating that a sale is to occur.

Usually during this time, inspections of the property and any necessary repairs to the property are coordinated with the parties and their real estate agents. If the contract calls for a property inspection, title agents and attorneys must determine when payment will be made. Buyers have monetary responsibility for the mechanical, electrical and structural inspections, while the pest or termite inspection, if necessary, is the seller's duty.

At this point in the process, the lender usually has the loan documents drafted by its own legal counsel. The title agent or attorney must coordinate the receipt of all the necessary legal documents including a note, mortgage or deed of trust, warranty deed and release in order to have them in time for the closing.

Ordinarily, hazard insurance (property, casualty insurance and flood insurance) is ordered by the buyer or his real estate agent; title agents and attorneys are required to have proof of the required amount of insurance before funding a loan.

Some lenders may require an impound, or escrow, account. The purpose of this account is to collect an estimated portion of insurance and taxes over the course of the year. The lender will then pay the insurance and taxes out of this account when the payments are due. This assures the lender that these payments will be made on time. Usually, several months of funds are collected at the time of closing to establish this account and then the tax and insurance payments are disbursed out of the account as they come due. In addition to the initial deposit, your prorated portion for a month of the estimated annual expenses will be added to the mortgage payment each month. In some cases, this requirement can be waived and the buyer will pay his own taxes and insurance as they become due. As each year passes, the amount paid to this account changes to cover increases or decreases in real estate taxes or hazard insurance.

Title search

A *chain of title* is the succession of deeds or other documents through which the title is traced from the present owner back to the original source of the title (the state or sovereign grant). A title search is the search of the public records, which include conveyances or deeds, mortgages or deed of trust liens, involuntary liens such as judgments or federal tax liens, wills, divorce decrees and other publicly filed documents that affect the ownership of the property. After these documents are found and copied, they are delivered to the title examiner or attorney for title examination.

Title examination

During the title examination phase, documents affecting the title are examined in order to verify the legal ownership of the property. All mortgage or deed of trust liens and encumbrances (such as leases) on the property and items such as restrictions, easements, setback lines and rights of way are documented. The summary of all the findings on the status of the title is called the title commitment, preliminary report, attorney's opinion or title report; the terms vary around the country.

Document preparation and/or request to produce

The following phase happens behind the scenes and generally, buyers and sellers don't have to concern themselves with it. Title agents or attorneys review the current ownership of the property to determine whether any curative work needs to be done. Curative documents are those that counteract or clear up defects, errors, omissions or irregularities in the chain of title. For example, a title search and examination may find that a mortgage loan, paid off by a home's previous owner, never had a lien release filed. To correct the public record, the title agent or attorney will file a curative document.

Depending on the state in which the closing takes place, either the title company or an attorney prepares the appropriate forms and any affidavits to close a sale. In some states, only attorneys are permitted to draft deeds, mortgages, affidavits, etc. (See the end of this chapter for states that require an attorney.)

At this point, the lender sends the title agent or attorney a set of closing instructions on the mortgage loan. These instructions specify what funds are to be collected on behalf of the lender and any requirements that the title agent or attorney must fulfill before closing and funding the loan. The title information and survey are reviewed again when the lender's instructions are received.

There are a variety of closing statements available for use. Most, if not all, residential real estate transactions involve the HUD-1 Settlement Statement from the U.S. Department of Housing and Urban Development. The HUD-1 is a federal form and is used in all 50 states plus the District of Columbia. (Please see page 150 for the HUD-1 form and page 152 for a line-by-line explanation.)

Scheduling the closing

The title agent or attorney schedules the closing according to the timetable in the sales contract. All parties generally want to close the transaction as soon as possible. The seller wants his or her proceeds, the buyer wants to move in and the real estate agents want their commission checks. It's best to leave some extra time for last-minute problems that may occur.

A few of the documents that can be expected in any real estate closing include:

- **Deed**: a document that conveys property from the seller/grantor to the buyer/grantee
- **Mortgage or Deed of Trust**: a document that pledges a property to a creditor for a debt
- **Real Estate Lien Note**: a written promise to pay a sum of money at a specific time or on demand (promissory note)
- **Release**: a document that discharges and releases the pledged property

Settlement/Closing the transaction

This is the culmination of all the previous stages! The seller signs the deed. The buyer signs the new mortgage. All other disclosures and documents are executed. The current lien is paid off and the new mortgage is executed and recorded in the county clerk's records. The seller, real estate brokers, attorneys, title company, escrow company, closing attorney and other disbursements required by the earnest money contracts are paid.

In most states, the parties to the real estate transaction, along with their respective real estate agents and attorneys, will be present at the closing. If the parties choose to close over a period of time rather than in a single meeting, the title agent or attorney may have the buyer close first so that all the funds can be available when the seller closes and disbursement can be completed.

All documents are explained to the extent allowed by law, executed by the appropriate party, signed and witnessed by the escrow or closing officer or notary public.

Title agents are not allowed to explain the meaning of the documents because that explanation may constitute an unauthorized practice of law. Although this limitation is not placed on closing attorneys, parties to the transaction will be counseled to seek out their own attorneys for any questions they might have. Each party should receive at least one copy of every pertinent executed document after closing.

Buyer and Seller Expenses

In general, the seller is responsible for all costs and expenses up to the point of the transfer of the title. Anything after that usually becomes the buyer's expense. The customary costs (which can be negotiated separately in the contract) paid by each party include:

Buyer Expenses	Seller Expenses
✓ Recording fees for deed and mortgage or deed of trust ✓ Loan fees, mortgagee's title insurance ✓ One-half of escrow or closing fee ✓ Attorney's fees for preparing necessary documents ✓ Hazard insurance premium for one year ✓ Escrow account for taxes and insurance (if required by lender) ✓ Prepaid interest ✓ Inspection fees (if applicable) ✓ Prorated portion of taxes	✓ Real estate commissions ✓ Recording fees for curative title matters ✓ One-half of escrow or closing fee ✓ Owner's title insurance premium in some states ✓ Attorney's fees for preparing necessary documents ✓ Prorated portion of taxes ✓ Any repairs called for in the contract ✓ Outstanding liens (for example, payoff of existing mortgage loan) ✓ Tax certificates ✓ Termite certificate (if required) ✓ Any loan charges called for in the earnest money or sales contract

Your Rights

The Real Estate Settlement Procedures Act (RESPA) is a consumer protection statute first passed in 1974. The purpose of RESPA is to help consumers become better shoppers for settlement (closing) services and to eliminate kickbacks and referral fees that unnecessarily increase costs.

RESPA requires that borrowers (buyers) receive disclosures at various times. Some disclosures spell out the costs associated with the settlement, outline lender servicing and escrow account practices and describe business relationships between settlement service providers.

RESPA also prohibits a person from giving or accepting anything of value for referrals of settlement service business related to a federally related mortgage loan and prevents a person from giving or accepting any part of a charge for services that are not performed. Finally, RESPA prohibits sellers from requiring buyers to purchase title insurance from a particular company.

For additional information about your protection under the RESPA statute, visit the U.S. Department of Housing and Urban Development (HUD) website at www.hud.gov.

After the Closing

After the funds are received, the escrow or closing officer balances the disbursement sheet. Payoffs are made on loans and other outstanding liens, the seller receives his or her proceeds, commission checks are cut for the real estate agents and all other miscellaneous fees and bills are paid. Simultaneously with the disbursement of the file, the documents are readied for recording and then sent to the appropriate county recorder.

Finally, the title policies are prepared and forwarded to the owner and lender after the recording information is received from the county recorder's office, at which time the escrow officer or closing officer can close the file.

The Closing Process on the Internet

With home buyers increasingly using the Internet to choose a real estate agent and view home listings, it was a logical step to move the actual closing process to the Internet as well. "Transaction management" is the system where all parties in a real estate deal have access to the contract information and documents over the Internet.

The most significant advantage to using such a system is that the buyer, seller and their respective real estate agents can see the informational services that have been ordered and keep up with the progress of the home sale transaction. Title agents and attorneys also may have access to a transaction management system either through their title insurance underwriter or through an independent service.

In a system such as Stewart's SureClose®, the seller or refinance customer, the buyer, real estate agents, lender, builder, inspector, title agent or attorney and other settlement service providers can communicate, view and send documents via a secure, password-protected website. The system displays step-by-step information about the transaction in an easy-to-use format that can be accessed by any PC. In addition, the system automatically sends notifications by e-mail or fax to the various parties when critical items are completed, cutting down on deliveries and phone calls.

The title agent or attorney sets the security on the site, so the buyer cannot see seller-specific documents and vice versa. With 24/7 access through a transaction management system, all parties can view their real estate transaction anytime, without concern about office hours or time zones.

State-by-State Guide

Are all closings throughout the U.S. handled in the same way? The basic answer to this question is "Yes!" While it is true the parties that handle the closings may differ throughout the United States, the fundamental closing practices are relatively unchanged.

New England States

In New Hampshire, Vermont, Maine, Massachusetts, Connecticut and Rhode Island, attorneys generally handle real estate closings.

East Coast States

As you work your way south through New York, New Jersey, Pennsylvania, Maryland and Virginia, you'll find that both title companies and attorneys are involved in real estate closings. The exceptions are North and South Carolina, West Virginia and Delaware, where attorneys handle all real estate closings.

Southern and Midwestern States

In some states, such as Alabama, Georgia and Mississippi and to a lesser extent, Kentucky, real estate closings are handled primarily by attorneys. The trend, however, is that title companies usually handle real estate closings in Southern and Midwestern states, including Florida, Tennessee, Ohio, Indiana, Illinois, Wisconsin and Michigan. In these states, attorneys represent the parties only when the properties are very expensive.

Western States

Ordinarily, the states located west of the Mississippi River utilize title companies to perform real estate closings, with the exception of Iowa where title insurance is not offered and attorneys, real estate companies and lenders perform closings. In Southern California and sometimes in Utah, Oregon and Alaska, escrow companies are used. These escrow companies are independent from title companies. The escrow company handles the real estate closing and the title company handles the search and examination of the title and the issuance of the title policies. The escrow company manages the closing pursuant to all the instructions they receive from the parties to the transaction.

If a title company handles a closing in California, it will issue general provisions (governing the way escrow will be processed and how disputes between parties will be addressed) to the parties along with its preliminary report or commitment to insure.

What is Title Insurance?

Purchasing several types of insurance coverage to protect your home and personal property is part of the closing process. Homeowner's or hazard insurance protects against loss from fire, theft or wind damage, while flood insurance protects against rising water. A unique coverage known as "title insurance" protects against hidden title hazards that may threaten your financial investment in your home.

Title insurance is not as well understood as other types of home insurance, but it's just as important. When purchasing a home, instead of purchasing the actual building or land, a buyer is really purchasing the title to the property—the right to occupy and use the space. That title may be limited by rights and claims (building restrictions imposed by local government, etc.) asserted by others, which may limit use and enjoyment of the property and even bring about financial loss. Title insurance protects against these types of hazards.

Other types of insurance that protect a home focus on possible future events and charge an annual premium, whereas title insurance protects against loss from hazards and defects that already exist in the title and is purchased with a one-time premium.

There are two basic kinds of title insurance, lender or mortgagee protection and owner's coverage. Most lenders require mortgagee title insurance as security for their investment in real estate, just as they may request fire insurance and other types of coverage as investor protection. For one premium, paid in advance, owner's title insurance lasts as long as the policyholders or their heirs have an interest in the insured property.

Title insurance offers financial protection against title hazards such as mistakes in public records, pending legal action against the property, or the sudden appearance of an unknown heir who claims ownership of the property, to name just a few. The title insurer will pay for defending against an attack on title and will either perfect the title or pay valid claims or diminution of value up to the face amount on the policy. Before you go to closing, ask about your title insurance protection and be sure to protect your home with an owner's title insurance policy.

The standard forms of title policies issued throughout most of the United States are the American Land Title Association (ALTA) policies. ALTA policies are used in 48 of the 50 states and the District of Columbia. Texas has its own forms of title insurance policies called ALTEX policies. Please note that there is no title insurance in Iowa.

Trust In The Professionals You've Chosen

Though the documentation and procedures to close a real estate transaction may seem challenging, there are seasoned professionals to guide you through the process. Take the time to choose your real estate agent, attorney/escrow officer, title officer and service providers wisely. Ask for recommendations from your friends and co-workers.

The most critical concern for a home buyer in the closing process is to obtain title insurance that protects against undisclosed claims to a property; most of the other procedures generally happen behind the scenes. The service providers will handle the creation of the necessary documents to close a real estate transaction, then it's up to you to review them and confirm they reflect the terms of the purchase and sales contract. Complete all the steps and before long, you'll be hanging your hat in your new home!

Moving Made Easy

Michael P. Fergus
President, SIRVA Global Moving Services (Retired)

Preparing for a Move

Of the estimated 43 million Americans who move each year, many attempt to tackle the project without adequate preparation. As a result, they're faced with unnecessary stress and a potentially miserable experience before the moving truck even pulls into their driveway.

While moving can be difficult, particularly when you relocate to another state, there are ways to minimize anxiety and make the process run smoothly. After spending more than 30 years in the moving industry, I have collected valuable "insider's tips." I also have found that no two moves are ever the same, so it's important to be an educated and prepared consumer.

Packing Your Life Away

If someone told you that you had less than 48 hours to pack all your belongings in an organized manner, panic would set in. Accordingly, there is no reason to wait until the week before your move to begin packing. Locate items that aren't necessities, like the food processor or foot massager collecting dust in the back of your closet, and start packing boxes several weeks before the move. Allowing enough time leads to a calmer and more organized packing process and an efficient unpacking experience.

Unless you're moving from a studio apartment, don't try to undertake all rooms at once. Pick one room and pack one area of that room at a time. That way, packing materials aren't taking over your home and you can stay focused on the task. It's also best not to mix items from different rooms in one box, even if the toaster does fit nicely with the bath towels.

On the top of each box, write a general description of the contents and indicate the room from which it came or where it will go in your new home. Affix colored stickers to boxes to designate certain rooms, and place a corresponding colored sign, sticker or even balloon outside the room in your new home where you want the color-coded boxes delivered. If you have personal items that are irreplaceable, like family photos or financial papers, it's best to personally transport them to minimize the risk of losing anything priceless during the move.

There's even a science to selecting boxes during the packing process. While it's tempting to use free boxes obtained from the grocery store, it's not always the best idea. These boxes are used, often dirty, and do not withstand the weight of most household items. Additionally, from a driver's perspective, the boxes' odd sizes also tend to make loading more difficult.

 Whether moving down the street or across the country, you can cut costs by eliminating items you don't really need. Clean out closets, drawers, garages and crawlspaces to make sure you aren't spending money to move items you no longer use or want. Hosting a garage sale or donating items to charities are two ways to help reduce the clutter and save money.

Once all your big items are packed, be sure to pack a small "survival" box with the essentials (flashlight, paper plates, cups, toilet paper, phone, soap and a couple of pans) and ask your van foreman to load it on the van last so that it will be unloaded first at your new home.

The Cast: Moving Professionals

It's important to know all the major players in your moving experience. Remember, the better educated you are about your move, the less likely it is that problems will occur.

Moving Counselor

When you've researched and selected a reputable moving company in your area, your first contact with the van line will be a moving counselor. A moving counselor is another title associated with a salesperson for a local moving company or agency. Like any good counselor, a moving counselor provides plenty of advice and support. He or she will most likely come to your home to explain the available services and survey everything in the residence that will be moved.

This a good time to assess items with special needs such as those that can't be moved (flammable cans of paint), require extra attention (pool table), or must be prepared before the move by you or a third party (draining a water bed, disconnecting a gas dryer, etc.). If you don't plan on taking an item, such as an old couch, make sure you tell your counselor so it's not included in the estimate.

The counselor will take the results from this survey and provide you with an estimate of costs and pricing options. If you haven't yet decided if you will do your own packing or hand the job over to a specially trained team, now's the time to ask the questions, get quotes, discuss moving valuation coverage and identify any additional expenses.

Once you've selected your mover and settled on a price, you'll be asked to sign an *Order for Service*, a contract that formally registers your move with the van line. While your moving counselor's job is mostly done, you still can contact the counselor if questions arise during final preparations.

Move Coordinator

The moving counselor will hand off all details of the move to the move coordinator, a person who registers your move and keeps in constant contact with the driver to finalize the relocation details. While the moving counselor can provide assistance, the move coordinator is a good primary contact if you have any questions on the status of your shipment while it's en route. Most reputable moving companies also offer toll-free customer service telephone numbers as a third point of contact and many allow you to track your shipment on their websites.

Van Foreman

After the move has been registered, the driver, or van foreman as he or she is also called since the role encompasses so much more than just driving, will handle the physical moving process. The van foreman will load the goods at origin, drive the van and deliver belongings into your new home. Don't be surprised if your van foreman arrives with a few helpers; this is typical during the loading and unloading process.

More detailed than the moving counselor's original survey, an *Inventory & Condition Report* of all items to be moved will be taken by the van foreman. In addition to tagging every individual carton or piece of furniture with the company's numbered labels, the driver will record each item and a description of any existing damage on an inventory form. Take the time to accompany your driver during the inventory process so you can point out any special concerns or handling considerations along the way. A driver should always pack and load carefully, but it doesn't hurt to stress items that need extra attention.

Before the loading process begins, your driver will ask you to sign the inventory to verify the condition of items prior to the move and to acknowledge which items are to be loaded in the van. The driver will also sign the contract and give you a copy. It's important to keep this contract with you when you arrive at your new home. Like any major purchase, it's always wise to have the documentation readily available in case it's needed.

A good van foreman will take special precautions to protect your home and its contents. This may include laying down "floor runners" to shield your carpets or padding banisters and doorways to avoid scratching woodwork or walls. The driver should wrap most of your furniture with specially constructed cloth pads to protect it from scratches, dents and dirt. All heavy items will be loaded on the bottom of the van and the remaining items will be tightly loaded in tiers inside the van to avoid jarring or shifting while on the road. If an item is particularly heavy, you may see your driver securing it with heavy nylon straps.

The next document you will need to sign is the *Bill of Lading*. The Bill of Lading authorizes the van line to transport your possessions and binds you to payment for the services performed; it also includes pickup and delivery schedules and the valuation and protection that you've selected. Moving is a hectic time and van lines understand that there are some situations when you can't be present to sign these contracts. If that scenario arises, make sure you arrange for a relative, neighbor or other responsible party to act as your agent and sign both the Bill of Lading and contract.

Once your documents are signed and the van is loaded, you and the van foreman should take one last walk through your house to ensure that nothing has been overlooked. Before the driver leaves, provide him with a phone number where you can be reached, either at your new residence or a cell phone number and an alternate contact.

While it's not a requirement to give any extra bonuses to your driver, it's customary to offer a soft drink or water and perhaps a light snack to your movers. Furthermore, a tip at origin and destination to recognize excellent service is also appropriate. Again, tipping is a personal decision and depending on the size of the load could range anywhere from $50-$300.

Destination Agent

For long distance moves, the destination agent is the middleman between you and your driver; he or she ensures that the unloading process runs smoothly and on schedule. Once you arrive in your new hometown, it's important for you to contact your destination agent so final delivery arrangements can be made. The driver will also contact the agent, move coordinator and the customer 24 hours prior to his expected arrival time so all parties involved know when to expect the delivery.

Most moving companies provide you with a two- to six-day period for delivery so you have a general idea of when to expect your items. Some companies offer their customers the "one-day load" option, a guaranteed unloading date predetermined by you and the moving company. If you cannot be at your new home for the unloading process, it may be necessary to unload your shipment into storage at an additional cost to you.

If you opted for unpacking services, your destination agent will arrange to unpack cartons at the time of delivery and will remove the used packing materials. Should you choose to do your own unpacking, you'll be responsible for the disposal of empty boxes and packing materials. The destination agent is also your primary contact to report any missing or damaged items after the unloading process is complete.

Moving into Your New Home

When the van pulls up, you should have payment ready. Unless approved billing or credit arrangements have been made in advance, the driver is required by law to collect payment for the move before your shipment can be unloaded at your new home.

Payment must be made in cash, certified or cashier's check, traveler's checks, money order payable to the van line or by credit card if approved in advance by the booking agent; most companies do not accept personal checks.

Once payment is made, you can expedite the unloading process by having a room-by-room furniture floor plan in mind. Tell the driver where you want things placed as they're unloaded and brought into your home. A clear vision of how you want your home to look before the movers arrive will ease stress for both you and the movers. This is also when those color-coded stickers on boxes come in handy.

The driver and crew should reassemble any items that they've disassembled at origin. Be sure to oversee the drivers as they unload and check off items from your Inventory & Condition Report as they come in. This is the time to note the condition of your belongings and report any damaged or missing items on the inventory.

 If your delivery is late because of the van line's delay, you should inquire with your destination agent about inconvenience claims for any reasonable out-of-pocket living expenses that you might have incurred.

Costs

Before 1980, determining the cost of an interstate move was simple because the government set standard moving rates or tariffs. All moving companies charged the same rate based on the total weight of the shipment and distance of the move. Shipment tonnage was determined by weighing the truck before and after the goods were loaded and this amount was multiplied by a predetermined rate. Since all moving costs were the same, van lines had to compete on service alone.

Today, tariffs are determined by the Household Goods Carriers Bureau, an industry organization, and approved by the U.S. Department of Transportation. This affords van lines some flexibility in determining charges, depending on the specific needs of the customer, the actual costs and prevailing market conditions.

On a local move, your cost will likely be based on an hourly rate and the amount of time it actually takes the movers to handle your shipment. If you're moving to a different state, the cost will be largely dependent on the weight of your shipment and the distance between origin and destination.

Always remember that it's possible for your estimate to be too low, meaning your items weigh more than the move counselor's approximation. If this should happen, you'll be expected to pay the original estimated cost and up to 10% of the overage upon delivery. The remaining balance for the overage will be due within 30 days. It's important when budgeting for the move to allow for this possibility.

For interstate moves, there is often an option of a binding estimate. With a binding estimate the price is guaranteed regardless of the actual weight of the items. However, choosing this option may result in paying slightly more than the actual weight. Other additional costs to consider are packing, unpacking, appliance servicing (detachment and hook-up) and additional labor fees if the van foreman and his crew have to contend with an especially long distance between the house and the van, or several flights of stairs when carrying your items. These are all topics you can discuss with your moving counselor prior to the actual move.

As with any purchase, you get what you pay for and the lowest price does not always mean the best value. Make sure you consider the company's reputation, reliability, performance record, claims settlement process and commitment to customer satisfaction.

Claims and Coverage

Everyone wants a move to go smoothly, but accidents sometimes happen resulting in damaged or even lost items. Therefore, it's important to select the proper coverage for your shipment.

In the moving industry, coverage is the valuation you place on your belongings that governs the mover's liability in case of loss or damage. Basic liability coverage entitles you to receive limited protection at 60 cents per pound per article. For example, if your new 40-pound, color TV is damaged, you'll be paid a maximum of $24 toward its repair or replacement. However, under full replacement value coverage, if an item is lost or damaged, your mover either repairs it to the pre-move condition, replaces it with a new item, or reimburses you for the cost of a replacement at today's price (not a depreciated cost).

Your moving counselor will run through all the pricing options. You should review your homeowner's insurance policy to determine whether especially valuable items such as crystal, antiques and collectibles are covered during a move. If you have items of an unusual nature or value, have them professionally appraised before the move.

STEP BY STEP
➲
In the unfortunate case that a claim has to be filed, follow these steps:

- Clearly record any losses or damages on the van foreman's inventory sheet before you sign it.

- Contact your destination agent or visit the van line's website for a claim form.

- File your claim promptly. While you have up to nine months to file, the more quickly you submit your claim, the faster the van line will be able to resolve the matter.

Rogue Movers

The deregulation of the moving industry and the closing of the Interstate Commerce Commission (ICC) in 1995, have led to a boom of smaller, regional companies with little government supervision to monitor their activities. The Internet has also changed the playing field. Consumers now have the ability to search online for companies that may offer prices that seem too good to be true; in many cases, they are just that!

The Transportation Department consumer hotline receives more than 5,000 complaints about movers each year. Many of these complaints focus on 'bait and switch' tactics with companies promising a low price and then, once they've packed and loaded the family's possessions, refusing to unload until the consumer pays a grossly inflated price. Essentially, these rogue movers hold the family's possessions hostage until they receive payment.

Unfortunately, there's little recourse for consumers in this situation. This is a civil matter, meaning you can sue the movers but the police cannot take action. In 2003, a major criminal investigation by the Department of Transportation and the F.B.I. resulted in the prosecution of 42 Florida-based rogue movers and 74 individuals who were involved in their operations.

Researching and selecting a reputable, established mover are ways to reduce the risks of inflated costs, late pickup and delivery and a poor claim settlement process. While investigating moving companies, keep in mind the following suggestions:

- ✓ Seek recommendations from people who have recently moved.

- ✓ Receive at least three price estimates before selecting a mover.

- ✓ Be suspicious of extremely cheap price quotes.

- ✓ Choose a moving company or van line that is certified by the American Moving & Storage Association (www.moving.org). These movers and van lines have voluntarily agreed to abide by a Code of Conduct that requires written estimates of charges, timely service and prompt response to claims and complaints. They also agree to arbitrate disputes of up to $5,000.

- ✓ Ask movers to explain their estimates in detail and request a hard copy.

- ✓ When moving interstate, ask for a copy of the consumer booklet, "Your Rights and Responsibilities When You Move" (www.fmcsa.dot.gov/factsfigs/moving.htm).

- ✓ Check out websites such as www.movingscam.com that identify rogue movers and offer advice on how to avoid them.

Make moving smartly a priority to eliminate unnecessary anxiety and problems. Research carefully, plan ahead and know your rights as a consumer. After all, there's a lot at stake—namely your personal, cherished belongings.

Reap the Rewards:
Tax Benefits

Robert J. Bruss
Tax Specialist and Real Estate Columnist

One of the many benefits of owning your own home is taking advantage of more deductions on your tax return. For the majority of homeowners, this is generally a simple exercise of deducting interest expense and real estate property taxes each year; however, when homes are used for businesses or as investments, the tax rules become challenging and additional research may be required. This chapter was designed to be of general interest and therefore, some of the information may not apply to your individual circumstances.

Home Sale Tax Rules

The Easy Eligibility Rules

If you are single, you can now exclude profits (capital gains) up to $250,000 on the sale of your principal residence. A qualified married couple can claim up to $500,000 tax-free home sale profits. To qualify, the sellers must have owned and occupied their principal residence an "aggregate" (total) of two of the five years before the home sale. Occupancy need not be continuous; nor, must the home be the sellers' principal residence at the time of sale.

If the seller owned and occupied the home for two years, and then rented it to tenants up to three years, the sale qualifies. This tax exemption can be used over and over again without limit, but it cannot be used more frequently than once every 24 months.

For a married couple, to claim up to $500,000 tax-free sale profits, only one spouse's name has to be on the principal residence title, but both spouses must meet the occupancy test. Or, if title is held in a living trust, new Internal Revenue Service (IRS) regulations clarify whether the full tax exemption is still available. The pre-1997 principal residence tax rules requiring the seller to buy a replacement home and the once-in-a-lifetime "over 55" age restrictions have been eliminated.

Partial Exemption After Less Than Two Years Ownership and Occupancy

A partial $250,000 exemption is available for home sales within less than 24 months of ownership and occupancy if the reason for the sale is: (a) change of employment location, which qualifies for the moving cost tax deduction; (b) health reasons for illness or to care for a family member; and (c) unforeseen circumstances.

A sale will be considered as occurring primarily because of "unforeseen circumstances" if any of these events occur during the taxpayer's period of use and ownership of the residence:

- death
- divorce or legal separation
- becoming eligible for unemployment compensation
- a change in employment that leaves the taxpayer unable to pay the mortgage or reasonable basic living expenses
- multiple births resulting from the same pregnancy
- damage to the residence resulting from a natural or manmade disaster, or an act of war or terrorism
- condemnation, seizure or other involuntary conversion of the property

Any of the first five situations listed must involve the taxpayer, spouse, co-owner, or a member of the taxpayer's household to qualify.

Partial exemptions exist for these situations based on the percentage of the 24-month occupancy time. For example, if you occupied your principal residence for 18 of the required 24 months, and sold due to one of the approved reasons, you would be entitled to 75% of the $250,000 (single) or $500,000 (married) principal residence sale exemption.

Special Rule for Divorced and Separated Couples

Inter-spousal real estate transfers, during the marriage or as part of a divorce or legal separation, are tax-free by using Internal Revenue Code 1041. However, if the couple retains co-ownership, but just one ex-spouse remains in the principal residence while the other ex-spouse lives elsewhere, each spouse can claim up to $250,000 tax-free profits if the spouse living in the home meets the two out of five years occupancy test when the home is sold. In other words, if the "in spouse" living in the principal residence qualifies for the $250,000 exemption, the "out spouse" not living in the residence also qualifies for up to $250,000 tax-free capital gains when the home is sold.

Rule for Sale of Adjoining Land

The 2003 IRS regulation changes now allow use of the principal residence exemption when adjoining vacant land is sold, even if the home isn't sold at the same time. The land sale qualifies for the $250,000 or $500,000 exemption if the adjacent parcel is sold within 24 months before or after the principal residence sale.

The Surviving Spouse Rule

A surviving spouse can claim up to $500,000 principal residence sale tax-free profits if the home is sold in the year of the other spouse's death. However, if the home is sold after the year of the spouse's death, the exemption reverts to $250,000.

How to Deduct Moving Costs

Are you one of the millions of renters and homeowners who changed residences last year? If so, your moving costs may be tax-deductible. Even if you don't itemize personal tax deductions, your moving costs might produce a deduction saving you hundreds—or even thousands—of tax dollars. Fortunately for those who don't itemize, the moving cost tax deduction is an "adjustment" subtraction from your gross taxable income rather than an itemized deduction.

To qualify, you must have changed your job location; however, it doesn't matter if you changed employers, stayed with the same employer, or became self-employed. Requirements include that your new job site is at least 50 miles further from your old home than your old job location. The distance from your new job location to your new residence is irrelevant.

EXAMPLE
➲ The drive from your old home to your old job location was five miles. To be eligible for the residence moving cost tax deduction, your new job site must be at least 55 miles (five plus 50) from your old home.

If you passed the first job location distance test, the second eligibility test requires employees to work full-time in the vicinity of their new job location for at least 39 weeks during the 52 weeks after their residence move. Either spouse can meet this test. Part-time employment or time spent job hunting doesn't count. The obvious purpose of this test is to prevent frequent tax-deductible moves.

The test for self-employed persons is tougher. They must work at least 78 weeks full-time in the vicinity of their new job location during the 104 weeks after their residence move. This test prevents self-employed students and hobbyists from deducting their moving costs although they work just a few hours each week. These work-time tests are waived for disability, job layoffs and the taxpayer's death.

Indirect Moving Costs Are Not Deductible

If a moving expense was not a direct cost of the residence move, it is not deductible. Examples of nondeductible indirect moving costs include pre-move inspection trip airfares, meals and lodging. Indirect costs for moving your chauffeur, nurse, butler, cook and housekeeper are also nondeductible. More examples of nondeductible indirect moving costs include a loss on the sale of your house, and residence sales or leasing commissions.

Direct Moving Costs Are Deductible Without Limit

Don't forget to deduct all direct household moving costs. If you drive from your old to new residence, you can deduct either 14 cents per mile or your actual out-of-pocket expenses, such as gasoline and oil, but not repairs and depreciation. In addition, parking and tolls are deductible. Direct expenses for hiring a moving van, shipping your pets, in-transit storage fees up to 30 days, insurance, and costs of moving your "personal effects" such as your horses, recreational vehicle and yacht, are also deductible.

How Employer Reimbursements
Affect Moving Cost Deductions

If your employer reimbursed your moving costs, you have neither moving cost deductions nor additional taxable income. However, if your actual direct moving costs exceeded the reimbursement, the excess moving costs are tax-deductible. If your employer reimbursed you a flat fee, which exceeds your direct moving costs, the excess is taxable income to you. Or, if your employer reimbursed you for indirect moving costs, such as non-deductible house hunting trips or for a loss on the sale of your house, that excess payment is taxable income to you, too.

Vacation and Second Home Tax Deductions

Do you own more than one home? Perhaps you, like millions of others, own a vacation or second home. Depending on your circumstances, you might be overlooking significant tax savings. If you keep careful tax records for both homes, you may be entitled to tax breaks during ownership and when you decide to sell. Just in case the IRS audits you, it's best to keep your residence tax records indefinitely.

Vacation or Second Home Benefits During Ownership

If you itemize your income tax deductions, your property taxes and mortgage interest are always deductible for your principal residence and a second or vacation home. There can be additional ownership deductions, though, depending on your personal use of your secondary home.

There are four possibilities:

1. No Personal Use Time

> If you didn't personally use your second home, other than for a few days for repair and maintenance work, and if it was rented or available for rent the rest of the year, then your rental income and expenses should be reported on Schedule E of your income tax returns. Schedule E is where your rent and applicable expenses such as mortgage interest, property taxes, insurance, utilities, repairs and depreciation deductions are calculated. You also can deduct reasonable travel expenses to inspect (but not occupy) your rental property.

2. Under 14 Days of Annual Rental

   If you rented your second or vacation home less than 14 days last year to tenants, regardless of how much rent you received, that rent is tax-free and need not be reported to Uncle Sam. You can still deduct the itemized mortgage interest, property taxes and any uninsured casualty loss (such as rain or snow damage) deductions.

3. Annual Personal Use Over 14 Days or 10% of Rental Days (if rented over 14 days last year)

   In this category of heavy personal use of a second or vacation home, but modest rental income, the rental income and expenses must be reported on Schedule E of your tax return. However, please note that any deductions exceeding rental income cannot be used to offset your ordinary taxable income. Unused losses are "suspended" for future tax-deduction benefits.

   The correct order for deducting expenses is mortgage interest, property taxes, uninsured casualty losses, operating expenses and depreciation. When mortgage interest, property taxes and uninsured casualty losses exceed the rental income received, however, these excess deductions should be itemized on Schedule A.

4. Annual Personal Use is Under 15 Days or 10% of the Rental Days

   This is a very desirable second home category because there is no limit to your tax-loss deductions against ordinary taxable income, subject to the $25,000 annual passive activity loss limit. To illustrate, suppose you rented your second home to tenants for 240 days last year, but you personally occupied it just 10 days. Because your annual personal use is less than 15 days, or 10% of the rental days, you can deduct up to $25,000 of qualifying losses against your ordinary income. However, Internal Revenue Code 183 says you must show a rental activity profit at least three of every five years in this category.

Deducting Home Business Expenses

An estimated 30 million U.S. taxpayers work full- or part-time from their owned or rented residences. Whether you are employed, working at home for the convenience of your employer or self-employed, you may be entitled to significant tax deductions for part of your household expenses. Deductible examples include a portion of your residence rent, utilities, insurance, repairs, painting, property tax, mortgage interest, depreciation and business equipment costs.

Home-Based Employees Have a Special Test

If you are an employee, such as an outside salesperson or a computer programmer working from your home, you have a special test to pass before you can deduct home business expenses. This test requires your work at home be for the "convenience of the employer." That means your employer doesn't provide suitable workspace and expects you to work primarily from your residence. However, if you rent part of your residence to your employer at a fixed amount, you won't qualify.

If you are an employee who prefers working from your home, such as a school teacher who enjoys grading papers and preparing lesson plans at home rather than at the school, you don't meet the "convenience of the employer" test. Some teachers, however, can meet this test if the schools where they work are not safe after school hours or the teachers are required to leave the premises after class hours.

The Primary Business Location Test
for Self-Employed Business Owners

Whether you operate a full- or part-time home business, you can probably qualify for the home business tax breaks allowed by Internal Revenue Code 280A.

If you are a real estate broker with a home office, you qualify if that is your only business location. However, if you are an independent contractor realty agent working for a real estate brokerage that provides you with a desk and a phone, your home office expenses aren't tax-deductible.

Full-time or part-time self-employed business owners must be able to prove their residences are either (1) used to meet or deal with patients, clients or customers, or (2) the principal business location used for administrative activity if they have no other fixed business location.

Even if you don't meet patients, clients or customers at your residence, you can deduct home business expenses when your residence is the principal business location used for administrative activity even though you spend most of your time working elsewhere. An example would be a plumber who receives customer calls at home and operates his business from a separate room, but spends most of his workday on service calls.

An "Exclusive Home Business Area" is Required

Assuming you passed the applicable home business use tests explained above, the next hurdle requires having an "exclusive home business area." It need not be a full room, but can be part of a room such as where you have your business equipment and supplies. You do not meet the requirements of the exclusive use test, however, if you use the area in question for both business and personal purposes. For example, using your dining room table to do business bookkeeping won't qualify if you also have family meals there. Another non-qualifying example is if you occasionally entertain business clients at your home, which is used by your family most of the time.

Home Business Area Square Footage
Determines Your Deductions

Whether you are self-employed or a qualified "convenience of the employer" employee using a designated home business area, the amount of your home business deductions depends on the business square footage area of your residence. IRS Form 8829 (Expenses for Business Use of Your Home) is the place to calculate your square footage and the percent of home business deductions.

EXAMPLE

➲ Suppose you own or rent an 1,800-square-foot house or apartment and your exclusive business area is 600 square feet. In this case, 33% of most of your household costs become tax-deductible. That means 33% of your homeowner's or renter's insurance, utilities, repairs, mortgage interest, rent and property taxes are deductible business expenses.

It's important to note that some home business costs are fully deductible. For instance, all home business phone expenses are fully deductible if you also have a separate personal telephone line. If you paint and renovate the business area, all expenses are deductible. Your business insurance premiums would also be fully tax-deductible.

Claim Business Depreciation If You Own Your Residence

Homeowners and condo owners who use part of their residence for qualified business use can claim depreciation for the exclusive business area of their residence. Using the above example in which the business area occupies 33% of the residence, you can depreciate 33% of your home's purchase price (excluding land value). However, IRS regulation 2002-142 states that when selling your principal residence, even its business area can qualify for the $250,000/$500,000 tax exemption of Internal Revenue Code 121.

Full-time and part-time business owners who operate primarily from their residence often overlook home business expenses. Qualified employees who are expected by their employers to work from their homes are often unaware of these tax-saving deductions. For more details on home business tax deductions, please consult a tax adviser.

Tax-Deferred Exchanges

Suppose you own a rental investment property in which you have accrued $100,000 equity from appreciation in market value and gradual pay-down of your mortgage balance. You would like to use that $100,000 to acquire more investment properties, however, if you sell, you will owe capital gains tax. Is there a way to use that $100,000 equity to buy more properties without paying tax on your sales profit? The answer is "yes." It's called a tax-deferred exchange, authorized by Internal Revenue Code 1031.

What is a Tax-Deferred Exchange?

To qualify for a tax-deferred exchange, a real estate investor ("up-trader") must trade "equal or up" in both price and equity for one or more qualifying "like kind" properties. The investor may not take out any taxable "boot" such as cash or net mortgage relief.

Most real estate is considered "like kind." For example, you can trade a rental house for an apartment building, or a warehouse for an office building. You can even trade your vacant investment land for a shopping center. Just about any real estate held for investment or for use in a trade or business is eligible. There is, however, an exception: Your personal residence and "dealer property," such as a homebuilder's inventory of houses, cannot qualify.

Why Trade Instead of Selling?

Since 1921, Internal Revenue Code 1031 has encouraged investment and business property owners to trade their properties to avoid paying capital gains tax. According to the IRS, a qualified tax-deferred exchange is viewed as one continuous investment.

CHECKLIST

➲ There are *at least* eight basic reasons for tax-deferred exchanges:

- pyramid your equity tax-deferred without paying capital gains tax
- get rid of a property which is hard to sell by trading for one that is more marketable
- eliminate or minimize the need for new financing on the acquired property
- acquire a property which is easier to manage
- defer part of your profit tax by trading down and taking back an installment sale mortgage
- acquire a property with greater profit potential, such as a "fixer-upper"
- receive tax-free refinance cash either before or after the exchange (but not as part of the trade)
- accept an unsolicited profitable purchase offer to sell your investment without paying capital gains tax.

How to Avoid Tax on the Sale of a Vacation or Second Home

When selling a vacation or second home, the $250,000 tax-free exemption doesn't apply because the second or vacation home is not the seller's principal residence. However, the best way to avoid tax on the sale of a vacation or second home is to convert it to a rental property and then make a Starker Tax-Deferred Exchange (see following section) using Internal Revenue Code 1031(a)(3) for another qualifying investment or business property.

Starker Exchanges Simplify Tax-Deferred Exchanges

In 1979, T.J. Starker won his famous U.S. Court of Appeals decision, which approved "delayed" tax-deferred exchanges. Starker sold his Oregon timberland to Crown-Zellerbach Corporation, which then held his sales proceeds until he located suitable replacement property to purchase with that money. However, upon audit, the IRS argued that it was a taxable sale. Starker paid the disputed tax and then sued for a refund. Fortunately for investors, Starker won. The result is Internal Revenue Code 1031(a)(3) authorizing indirect delayed tax-deferred exchanges. Starker Exchanges have become the most popular type of tax-deferred exchange.

Time Limits Apply to Starker Exchanges

To qualify for a Starker delayed tax-deferred exchange, the sales proceeds for the investment or business property must be held in trust beyond the up-trader's "constructive receipt" by a qualified third-party intermediary. Most title insurance and bank trust departments can handle Starker exchanges. After the sale of the old investment property, the up-trader has 45 days to designate the qualifying replacement property to be purchased with the sales proceeds. IRS regulations permit up to three possible property acquisitions to be named. The up-trader then has 180 days from the sale date to complete the acquisition.

IRS Legalizes Reverse Exchanges

In 2000, the IRS issued Revenue Procedure 2000-37, which approved "reverse exchanges." A reverse exchange overcomes the short 45-day Starker replacement property designation time limit by permitting acquisition of the qualifying replacement property before the old property is sold. However, title to the reverse exchange replacement property must be taken in the name of the third-party intermediary until the up-trader's old investment or business property is sold.

Making the Most of Home Ownership

With all the tax benefits available to home buyers and investors, it is well worth preparing IRS itemized schedules to maximize your deductions. However, before acting on any matter contained in this chapter, you should consult with a tax adviser.

Setting Goals to Buy the Home of Your Dreams

Brian Tracy
Motivational Speaker &
Best-Selling Author

The potential of the average person is like a huge ocean unsailed, a new continent unexplored, a world of possibilities waiting to be released and channeled toward some great good.

—Brian Tracy

For the past fifty years, buying a home has been an attainable goal for almost everyone. Today, diverse lending programs and creative financing keep home ownership within reach in spite of rising prices. As with all worthwhile endeavors, buying your first or your next home requires careful planning, a long-term vision and personal growth. With expert guidance and perseverance, the home of your dreams can, and will, be yours.

Your Personal Growth and Development Vision

Create a long-term vision for yourself in the area of personal growth. Project forward five or 10 years and imagine that you are developed fully in every important part of your life. Idealize and see yourself as outstanding in every respect. Refuse to compromise on your personal dreams.

What kind of work would you be doing? What level of skill or ability would you have in your field? What level of status and prestige would you have attained as the result of your superb performance at what you do? How would you think and feel about yourself as a result of being one of the very best at what you do? If you had no limitations at all, what would be your vision for how you would develop yourself in the months and years ahead?

The Path to Your New Home is Paved with Goals

STEP BY STEP
➲

Now take your vision and crystallize it into specific goals. Here is a good way to start:

Take out a piece of paper and write down 10 goals that you would like to achieve in the area of personal and professional development in the months and years ahead. Write in the present tense, exactly as if you were already the person you intend to be. Determine exactly what you want to be able to do. Decide who you want to become. Describe exactly what you will look like when you become truly excellent in your field and in your personal life. Picture the house of your dreams you will be living in when you achieve these goals.

Then, review this list of 10 goals and select the one goal that, if you achieved it, would have the greatest positive impact on your life and on your career. Put a circle around that goal and move that goal to a clean sheet of paper.

Create a schedule for achieving this goal. Set deadlines for achieving certain benchmarks. Set sub-deadlines as well. Make a list of everything you can think of that you will have to do to achieve personal excellence in that area. Organize your list into a plan by setting priorities for each of the items. Gather the books, materials, equipment and other resources you will need to begin to work on yourself and your goal.

Take immediate action on at least one item in your plan to get the process started. Resolve to do something every day until you are successful in that area. Never stop working on yourself until you become the kind of person you would most like to be.

Upgrade Your Personal Knowledge and Skills

Set specific measures for each of your goals. If your goal is to excel in your field and ultimately, to purchase a three-bedroom, two-bath home on a particular street in a specific upscale neighborhood, decide how you can measure your progress and evaluate your success. Perhaps you can use as a measure the number of hours you study in your field each week. Perhaps you can measure the number of books you read or the number of audio programs you listen to. Perhaps you can measure your progress by the number of appointments you get or the number of sales you make as the result of your growing skills.

Compare yourself against these measures regularly. The more precise your measures and the more you pay attention to them, the better you will become in that area and the greater progress you will make.

Here are some key goal questions you can ask and answer for yourself:

- What additional knowledge do you need to be the best in your field?

- What additional skills must you acquire to do your work in an excellent fashion?

- What subjects do you need to study and master?

- What skills can you improve that will help you the most in your work or career?

- What are the key result areas of your job?

- What is your plan to acquire these critical skills?

- What is your plan to excel in each of these areas?

- What one skill or ability, developed and done in an excellent fashion, would have the greatest positive impact on your life and your career?

You first determine your values, vision, goals and the knowledge and skill you will need to achieve them. You choose the ways in which you will measure your progress toward each of them. You then do something every day that makes you better in some way. You read, take courses, listen to audio programs, practice your new skills and never stop improving.

Winning Personal Development Habits

Select the specific habits and behaviors you will need to practice every day to become the person you want to become. These could be the habits of clarity, planning, thoroughness, studiousness, hard work, determination and persistence.

Perhaps the most important single quality for success is self-discipline. Twentieth-century thinker-writer Elbert Hubbard defined self-discipline as "the ability to make yourself do what you should do, when you should do it, whether you feel like it or not." Napoleon Hill of *Think and Grow Rich* fame called self-discipline "the master key to riches."

Every day, and every hour of every day, you have to practice self-discipline. You have to command yourself to do what is right, necessary and important, or you will end up doing what is fun, easy and unimportant. Self-discipline is the quality that enables you to choose to do the most important task, whether you feel like it or not, and stick to it. Self-discipline is an indispensable quality of all high-performing men and women.

Create Your Daily Personal Growth and Development Activity Schedule

There are seven disciplines you must develop if you want to achieve all that is possible for you. You can learn these disciplines through practice and repetition until they become automatic.

STEP BY STEP ➲

1. Daily goal setting

   Every morning, take three to five minutes to write out your top 10 goals in the present tense. Get a spiral notebook for this purpose. By writing out your 10 goals at the beginning of each day, you will program them deep into your subconscious mind. This daily goal writing will stimulate your mind and make you more alert. Throughout the day, you will see opportunities and possibilities to move more rapidly toward your goals.

2. Daily planning and organizing

   Take a few minutes, preferably the night before, to plan out every activity of the coming day. Always work from a list. Always think on paper. This is one of the most powerful and important disciplines of all for high performance.

3. Daily priority setting

    The essence of all time management, personal management and life management is contained in your ability to set the proper priorities on the use of your time. Select the most valuable and important task you could possibly do and start work immediately on that task. This is essential for high performance.

4. Daily concentration on your highest-value activities

    Your ability to work single-mindedly on your most important task will contribute as much to your success as any other discipline you can develop.

5. Daily exercise and proper nutrition

    Your health is more important than anything else. By disciplining yourself to exercise regularly and to eat carefully, you will promote the highest possible levels of health and fitness throughout your life.

6. Daily learning and growth

    Your mind is like a muscle. If you don't use it, you lose it. Continuous learning is the minimum requirement for success in any field.

7. Daily time for the important people in your life

    Relationships are everything. Be sure that in climbing the ladder of success, you do not find it leaning against the wrong building. Build time for your relationships into every day, no matter how busy you get.

These seven disciplines will ensure that you perform at the highest level and get the greatest satisfaction and results from everything you do.

The 1,000 Percent Formula

There is a simple, practical, proven self-development formula that you can use to double your income in the years ahead. It's an effective formula I developed early in my career, and I have passed it on to thousands of people who practice it daily and report extraordinary improvements in their lives. Try it and see for yourself.

The 1,000 Percent Formula is based on the law of incremental improvement. This law states, "by the yard it's hard, but inch by inch, anything's a cinch."

No matter how excited or determined you are, change and progress take place slowly. We do not usually make significant and lasting changes in quantum leaps. All permanent change is progressive, over a long period of time. This type of change takes patience and discipline.

Here is a question for you: Is it possible for you to increase your overall productivity, performance and output by 0.1% in the next 24 hours? In other words, could you become one-thousandth (0.1%) more productive over the next 24 hours if you really wanted to?

The truth is that you could probably become 0.1% more productive right now, in a couple of minutes, just by working on a single high-value task. By setting goals and priorities and by focusing on higher-value activities, many people could double or triple their overall productivity in the next 24 hours if they really wanted to.

If you continually learn, study and upgrade your skills, clarify and reclarify your goals, set better and clearer priorities and focus on progressively more valuable tasks, you can increase your overall productivity performance and output by 0.1% each day, day after day, indefinitely. Every effort you make to be more productive in one area tends to improve your performance in every other area at the same time. You will get better and better results, in less time, the more you practice.

If you become 0.1% more productive each day, five days per week, at the end of a week you will be 0.5% more productive. At the end of four weeks, you will be 2% more productive (4 x 0.5 = 2). At the end of 52 weeks, you will be 26% more productive than you were at the beginning of the year (13 x 2 = 26).

This is where the compounding effect of new knowledge and skill begins to work. Because we live in a merit-based society, as you improve your overall performance, your income eventually will rise to match the value of your contribution.

STEP BY STEP ➔ Here are the seven steps in the 1,000 Percent Formula:

1. Before you end your workday or before you go to bed, make a list of everything you have to do the next day. Plan every day in advance. This enables your subconscious mind to work on your list while you sleep. Often, when you awake, you will have ideas and insights that will help you to achieve your daily goals faster and more efficiently.

2. Arise two hours before your first appointment and read for one hour in your field. This hour is called the "Golden Hour," and it sets the tone for the rest of the day. Leave the television off; put the newspaper aside. Invest the first 60 minutes in yourself and in your mind. This first hour is the rudder of your day.

3. Review and rewrite your major goals in your spiral notebook each day before you start off. Always write in the present tense, as though you had already achieved them. This programs your subconscious mind to be alert to opportunities to achieve your goals all day long.

4. Always concentrate on the most valuable use of your time. Remember, your most important task is the one that can have the greatest positive impact on your life. Begin on that task first thing in the morning.

5. Turn your car into a mobile classroom and listen to great educational audio programs in your car. This activity is so powerful that it alone can give you your 1,000 percent increase in the years ahead.

6. Ask two questions after every experience: "What did I do right?" and "What would I do differently?" These questions enable you to learn and grow more rapidly from everything that happens to you.

According to the law of concentration, whatever you dwell upon grows in your experience. Whatever you pay attention to increases in your life. Whatever you focus on, you tend to do better. When you analyze each experience by asking, "What did I do right?" and "What would I do differently?" you program yourself to perform even better in each subsequent experience. These questions enable you to extract the maximum number of lessons out of each thing you do and to learn at an accelerated rate.

The best news of all is that when you are concentrating on what you did right and what you would do differently, your mind becomes positive, productive and creative. You become more motivated and more eager to try new things. You become even more likely to apply the insights you derived from your previous experiences.

7. The seventh and final ingredient of the 1,000 Percent Formula is for you to treat everyone you meet like a million-dollar customer. Treat the people you work with the same way you would treat a valuable customer of your firm. Treat each prospect or customer as if that person had already purchased one million dollars of your company's product or service and was thinking of doing it again. Also, treat the people at home as though they were the most valuable people in the world to you, because they are.

Make Your Personal Growth and Development Action Commitment

You are your most precious resource. Your earning ability is your most valuable asset. Invest every day in improving yourself as a person and increasing your ability to earn even more. Most people who are earning $250,000 annually today started off earning $25,000 or less.

By setting goals, creating a schedule to achieve them, resolving to take a step toward success every day and monitoring your progress, you are on your way to realizing your full potential. Decide today to develop yourself to the point where you can achieve every financial and personal goal you ever set and become everything you are capable of becoming. You should be in your dream house in no time!

Home Buying Highlights

Home Buying 'To Do' List

TO DO	DONE
Read *Home Buying by the Experts*	✓
Get a copy of your credit report and correct any errors	
Pay down credit card balances to reduce your debt	
Take inventory of your finances	
Determine how much you *can afford* to pay for a home	
Decide how much you *want to spend* for a home	
Research mortgage terms and rates	
Shop for a mortgage loan on the Internet	
Complete mortgage loan applications	
Get pre-approved for a loan	
Investigate neighborhoods where you want to look for a house	
Select two or three neighborhoods that meet your requirements	
Find a real estate agent who specializes in the neighborhoods you've chosen	
Work with your agent but also shop for a home online	
Visit homes for sale and make notes	
Get your agent's help in evaluating the asking price of homes you like	
Decide how much to offer for the home you want	
With the help of your real estate agent, write a Purchase Agreement	

TO DO	DONE
Hire an experienced inspector to examine your prospective home	
Accompany your inspector during the inspection and ask questions	
Get agreement on repairs to be made by the seller	
Inspect repairs and handle other details prior to closing day	
Hand over a certified check at closing and pick up the deed to your home	
Plan for your move well in advance	
Meet with your tax advisor to discuss deductions	
Enjoy your new home!	

Down Payment Strategies

Brian Yui
CEO, HouseRebate.com

Saving for a down payment, while second-nature to some, is a real challenge for a large number of home buyers. Below, you'll find some tried and true strategies to make saving a cinch.

1. Keep the mindset that you will own a home and consistently visualize your down payment amount.

2. Start reviewing your financial situation to determine which expenses you can reduce or eliminate.

3. Keep a separate savings or investment account for your down payment. Don't tap into this account until you are ready to buy.

4. Pinch a few pennies. Stock up when there is a sale on products that you normally use such as toothpaste, paper towels or canned goods. Buying a $2 item that is on sale for $1 is a guaranteed 100% return on your money. That beats the stock market any day!

5. Clip coupons for products that you normally buy and look for supermarkets that will double your savings. Each dollar adds up. Most coupons arrive in your Sunday paper or can be found online on the newspaper's website.

6. If you can cook, eat at home more often. Those restaurant tabs can add up.

7. Do without your daily drink purchased at the coffee shop. Saving at least $2 a day on gourmet coffee will enable you to put an extra $60 toward a mortgage payment or an extra $10,000 in increased loan balance.

8. Consider shopping at discount stores such as Costco or Sam's Club where you can buy in bulk. Warning: Avoid buying quantities that you will not use.

9. Opt for an automatic savings withdrawal from your paycheck. It's easier to save when you don't have money burning a hole in your pocket.

10. When you order services, always get three bids. Assuming the quality is the same, pick the lowest price one.

11. Earn money in your spare time. Consider starting a part-time business on the Internet. Check out www.marketingtips.com for guidance.

12. Pay off your credit cards monthly. Don't incur those high credit card interest rates.

13. Pay cash for everything you buy and stick with your budget. If you have more self-control, consider using a credit card that offers cash back like the Discover card. Only do this if you pay off your cards monthly.

14. When buying items on the Internet, consider using online shopping bots such as www.mysimon.com, www.shopping.com, www.pricegrabber.com, or www.shopzilla.com. Shopping bots compare prices of items from several different websites and include tax and delivery.

15. If you're getting married, skip the usual gifts in favor of a down payment registry.

The Smart Buyer's Checklist

There's a lot to take in when you preview a home. After you've narrowed your choices, use this convenient side-by-side comparison chart to evaluate the interior and exterior features of your top home choices. Some of the features may not be important to you, but your assessment must take future buyers into consideration.

Exterior

	House A	House B
Address		
Asking Price/ Value Range		
Home Type :		
Single family		
Condo		
Town house		
HOA/Other fees		
Age of home		
Number of stories		
Curb Appeal		
Notes		

	House A	House B
LOT FEATURES		
Size (sq. ft./acres)		
Corner Lot		
Land Slope:		
Toward house		
Away from house		
Drainage		
Sidewalks		
Storm Drain		
Streetlights		
Landscaping		
Garage (# of cars)		
Carport		
Driveway:		
Paved		
Gravel		
Straight		
Circular		
Utilities:		
Above ground		
Underground		
Fenced/Walled Yard		
Backyard Size		
Street Location:		
Busy		
Quiet		
Notes		

	House A	House B

HOUSE FEATURES

Exterior Walls:

Brick/Wood/Siding/
Stone

Condition

Roof Material:

Shingle/Shake/Tile

Age of Roof

Gutters

Porch

Deck

Patio

Outdoor lighting

Security Lighting

Built-in BBQ

Outdoor Fireplace/Firepit

Swimming Pool

Hot Tub

Drip/Sprinkler System

Tennis Court

Basketball Court

Storm Windows

Screens

Antenna/Cable TV

Other

Notes

Location

	House A	House B
Urban/Suburban/Rural		
Growth Rate		
Property Values: (increasing, stable, declining)		
Housing Demand		
Avg. Single Family Home Price:		

➲ DEMOGRAPHICS

	House A	House B
Owner Occupancy %		
Average Age		
Median Income		

➲ NEIGHBORHOOD

	House A	House B
Proximity to Workplace		
Proximity to Shops		
Proximity to Schools		
Proximity to Hospitals		
Proximity to Churches, synagogues, etc.		
Parks/Recreation		
School District Rating		
Public Transportation		
Crime		
Police Presence		
Appearance of Homes		
Noise Level:		
Days		
Nights		

Interior

	House A	House B
Sq. ft. of Living Area		
Cost per sq. ft.		
Number of Rooms		
Number of Bedrooms		
Number of Bathrooms		
Attic		
Basement		
Closets		
Bathroom Fixtures		
Insulation		
Plumbing		
Electrical		
Future Marketability		

KITCHEN EQUIPMENT

	House A	House B
Cabinets (quality)		
Counters (space)		
Refrigerator (cu. ft.)		
Oven/Range		
Range Hood/Fan		
Disposal		
Dishwasher		
Trash Compactor		
Microwave		

	House A	House B

⮌ BATHROOM FEATURES

Bathroom One
(shower, tub)

Bathroom Two
(shower, tub)

Bathroom Three
(shower, tub)

⮌ LIVING AREA

Foyer/Entryway Size

Living Room Size

Separate Dining Room

Family Room/
Great Room

Office

Bonus Room

Flooring (hardwood,
carpet, tile, other)

⮌ BEDROOMS

Master Bedroom

Second Bedroom

Third Bedroom

Fourth Bedroom

Flooring (hardwood,
carpet, tile, other)

	House A	House B

BASEMENT

Finished/Unfinished   _____   _____

Exterior Entrance   _____   _____

Sump Pump   _____   _____

Dampness/Mildew   _____   _____

Evidence of Mold   _____   _____

LAUNDRY/UTILITY ROOM

Separate Laundry Area   _____   _____

Equipment (condition)   _____   _____

ATTIC

Finished/Unfinished   _____   _____

Insulation   _____   _____

OTHER FEATURES

Fireplaces   _____   _____

Central Air
Conditioning   _____   _____

Hot Water Heater
(gallons, age)   _____   _____

Furnace (size, age)   _____   _____

Heating (gas, electric,
oil, age)   _____   _____

Heat Pump (age)   _____   _____

Ceiling Fans (number,
in which rooms)   _____   _____

Average Outlets per
Room   _____   _____

Expenses

	House A	House B
Home price		
Approximate Insurance		
Real estate taxes		
HOA/Special Assessments		
Utilities		
Approximate Overall cost		

Notes:

_____

_____

_____

_____

_____

_____

_____

_____

_____

_____

_____

_____

Evaluating the interior and exterior of a home you might want to buy is a great way to assess the quality, condition and features. Always take into consideration your 'gut' reaction to a home. A perfectly maintained house might leave you cold while one in some disrepair could cry out to you for tender loving care and feel just like home. Whatever the case may be, there is no substitute for a professional inspector with a trained eye who will prepare a report advising you exactly what you're getting into!

How to Make Offers in 'Hot Markets'

Coping with Multiple Offers on Your Dream Home

Don't underestimate the influence of emotion when it comes to buying and selling a home. Though commercial real estate ultimately comes down to dollars and cents, the residential market is often more subjective.

Homeowners, who've raised children and celebrated many milestones in the same house for years, care deeply about their homes and neighborhoods. A potential buyer may be able to edge out the competition by demonstrating to the seller that he's become emotionally attached to the home and by revealing some personal information so that the seller considers the buyer's feelings.

Of course, coming up with the purchase price is the bottom line. However, since few buyers pay cash for homes, qualifying for a loan and meeting financial obligations are the foundations of most transactions. Including reference letters from accountants with an offer may help persuade a homeowner to sell to you. Additionally, a pre-approval letter from a financial institution indicating that the buyer is pre-approved for a loan at or exceeding the amount in the offer can be a dealmaker.

Another good idea is to make an offer as close to the listing price as possible. Offering an amount above the purchase price in the event that you have your heart set on a home may be a good strategy and should be considered carefully.

Custom Terms Can Cinch a Deal

After price and financing, contractual terms can make or break a deal. Some sellers are interested in long escrows and others in short ones and many sellers' agents may prefer to work with a particular escrow or title firm that they feel is reputable and efficient.

Perhaps an increase in the deposit may entice a seller. For example, a buyer could offer up to 10% instead of the customary 3%. A buyer's agent should do some investigation to discover what might encourage a particular homeowner to sell to his or her clients.

An eager seller most likely will turn down an offer that makes the purchase contingent upon the buyer selling his home. Instead, to increase your odds of the seller accepting your offer, consider selling your house before searching for another home.

Dos & Don'ts for the Motivated Buyer

CHECKLIST **Do...**

➔ ✓ try to sell your home first.

✓ have the broker submit the offer in person.

✓ make yourself available from the time the offer is submitted through its conclusion.

✓ contemplate reducing or eliminating the standard contingencies in the purchase agreement.

✓ agree to the seller's title and escrow companies whenever possible.

✓ compose a letter to the seller explaining why you are right for this house and include a photo of your family.

✓ supply evidence of job history and proof of funds so that the seller will feel certain of your ability to purchase the property.

✓ respond in a timely manner to all counter offers and requests for further information.

✓ have your agent develop a relationship with the listing agent to get the inside track on the best offer strategy.

Don't...

x   choose a novice; find a local agent with a good reputation.

x   delay in submitting an offer to check minor details; you can always do your research during the due diligence period.

x   submit an offer wrought with contingencies.

x   propose to purchase items not included in the contract unless you know the seller is willing to consider such an offer.

x   speak negatively about the home or talk about renovation in the presence of a seller or seller's agent.

x   insult an owner by offering less than the asking price on a fairly priced home.

Top 10 Mistakes
Home Buyers Make

1. **Looking at Houses You Can't Afford**

   Talk to a financial institution to determine what size mortgage fits your income and circumstances. Once you know what that equates to in home prices, begin your search. Don't waste time and energy looking at homes that are unrealistic.

2. **Not Having a Loan Approval**

   Remember, pre-qualification and pre-approval are different. Having a loan approval in hand is a lot more powerful when presenting offers to sellers. It should put you at the top of the list if there are competing offers from buyers who aren't pre-approved.

3. **Not Checking a Builder's Reputation**

   Like all other professionals, builders have varying track records. While some may have a golden reputation, others might have lawsuits pending against them, a history of shoddy workmanship or other problems. They won't necessarily disclose this to you, so do your homework.

4. **Not Hiring a Professional Home Inspector**

   A professional home inspector may point out major defects and items that need repair, which the average person might not notice. It's well worth the inspection fee, as unforeseen or unnoticed problems can be costly. In addition, a mold inspection is highly recommended; most insurance policies don't include coverage for mold damage.

5. Bad Timing

There are many considerations with timing. If you've been renting until now, be sure that you time your move to coincide with the end of your lease. Don't sign another yearlong lease if you expect to buy a home before the period expires.

6. Not Buying When You Can Afford To

Chances are there's a home out there in your price range and a mortgage program that will work for you. The longer you wait, the more money it will cost you in tax savings and equity. So, buy as soon as you are able but remember it takes at least three to four years to recoup buying and selling costs, which run from 6% to 8% of the home's price. Accordingly, if you sell your house before it appreciates 6% to 8%, you may experience a loss.

7. Buying a Home That's the Wrong Size

Think about your future needs. Is your family growing? Do you want a home office? Will an elderly parent need to live with you in the future? Will the existing plot of land accommodate expansion?

8. Choosing the Wrong Loan

How long you plan to stay in a home is a factor in selecting the right loan. If you might move within five or 10 years, a variable-rate loan or a short-term fixed loan may save you money; the rates are generally lower than the 30-year fixed rate.

9. Underinsuring Your Home

Make sure that you obtain enough insurance to cover the replacement value of your home. As the cost of replacing a home increases, be sure to increase your coverage so that you do not come up short if there is a casualty.

10. Buying in the Wrong Location

Test-drive your daily commute, check crime reports for the area and ensure that schools and services are adequate. Don't forget about resale value: Most first-time home buyers move within seven years of ownership. Practice the famous real estate axiom: location, location, location!

The 10 Most Frequently Overlooked Tax Deductions

Robert J. Bruss
Tax Specialist and Real Estate Columnist

I f you own a house, apartment, condo or town home, you might be among the millions of homeowners who neglect to claim all the tax deductions to which you are entitled. Uncle Sam strongly encourages home ownership by awarding special tax breaks not available to non-owners, but it's up to homeowners to use these tax benefits to their maximum advantage.

Not every deduction will apply to every homeowner, however, it's important to know about each one and claim all the appropriate ones. Using just one or two of the following forgotten tax breaks can save hundreds—sometimes thousands—of tax dollars.

1. **If you bought a home this year, deduct your principal mortgage acquisition loan fee.**

   If you paid a loan fee (usually called "points") to obtain your home mortgage, that loan fee qualifies as an itemized interest deduction in the year of home purchase. Each point equals 1% of the amount borrowed. For example, if you obtained a $100,000 home acquisition mortgage and paid a two-point loan fee to lower your mortgage's interest rate, that $2,000 fee qualifies as an itemized interest deduction.

The general rule is that for each one-point loan fee paid, the lender will reduce the loan's interest rate by 1/8%. That's why smart home buyers pay a one- or two-point loan fee to (a) reduce their loan's interest rate and (b) deduct the loan fee in the tax year of principal residence purchase. Be sure to double-check the IRS Form 1098 sent to you in January by your home loan lender. If it did not include the loan fee points, be sure to itemize them anyway on Schedule A of your income tax return. Your proof of payment usually will be on the loan closing papers received at the time of home purchase.

2. **Deduct home mortgage refinance fees over the life of the mortgage.**

If you refinanced your home mortgage and paid loan fee points to obtain the loan, those points are not deductible in the year of payment. Instead, you can deduct them over the life of the mortgage.

To illustrate, suppose you paid $1,000 loan fee points to refinance your home loan with a new 30-year mortgage. The tax result is for each of the next 30 years you will have an itemized $33.33 deduction ($1,000 divided by 30). For most homeowners, however, rather than paying loan fee points when refinancing, they are usually better off obtaining a no-fee refinanced mortgage and paying a slightly higher tax-deductible interest rate.

3. **Deduct undeducted loan fees from a prior home loan refinance.**

If you refinanced your home loan, perhaps for the second or third time to take advantage of record-low interest rates, any undeducted mortgage loan fees from your prior home loan refinance can be deducted in full in the year of the refinance. For example, suppose you had $900 of undeducted loan fee points from a prior refinance. Because you refinanced to pay off that old mortgage, the full $900 became deductible on your income tax return in the year of the refinance.

4. **Deduct any home mortgage pre-payment penalty.**

Whether you sold your home or refinanced its mortgage, if you paid a mortgage pre-payment penalty, don't forget to claim it as an itemized Schedule A income tax deduction. Be sure to double-check the IRS Form 1098 received from your lender because it might not include the pre-payment penalty.

5. **Deduct prorated mortgage interest in the year of home sale or purchase.**

   If you bought a home and took over its existing mortgage payments from the prior owner (called "assuming" or buying "subject to" the mortgage), the mortgage interest was prorated between the buyer and seller in the month of purchase. This proration is usually calculated on the closing settlement statement. Even if the other party actually paid the mortgage payment for the month, you are entitled to deduct your share of the prorated mortgage interest as an itemized deduction on your income tax return.

6. **Deduct your share of prorated property taxes if you bought or sold your home.**

   Whether you bought or sold your home, you are entitled to deduct your share of the prorated property taxes, even if the other party actually paid the local tax collector's bill. Your share of the prorated tax bill should be shown on your closing settlement statement. Although most homeowners remember to deduct their property taxes, it's easy to forget this deduction because often your only evidence of payment is on the closing statement.

7. **Deduct pre-paid mortgage interest and property taxes.**

   For those homeowners looking for every possible income tax deduction, pre-paying mortgage interest and property taxes can be a great tax savings. The only drawback, however, is you must have made the pre-payments by December 31.

   Double-check your mortgage lender's IRS Form 1098 to be sure it included any prepaid mortgage interest for the January payment that you paid to the lender in December. If you prepaid your property taxes prior to the year they're due, you should have either a cancelled check or other evidence you prepaid. Not all property tax collectors allow early payments, but if yours does, it can be a great tax saver.

8. **Deduct property taxes paid from your escrow impound account.**

   If your mortgage payment includes a monthly escrow or impound account payment for one-twelfth of your annual property tax bill, double-check to be certain your mortgage lender remitted your property taxes to the tax collector on time. Unfortunately, many mortgage lenders forget to pay these important tax bills promptly. Just because you paid your escrow impound payment on time does not make the full amount paid tax-deductible. Only the amount actually remitted to the property tax collector in the tax year qualifies as an itemized deduction for your primary or secondary home.

9. **Deduct ground rent payments if your home is on leased land.**

Several million homeowners are not aware of this special tax break concerning an owned residence located on leased land. To qualify, your situation must meet the tax law's exact requirements.

Internal Revenue Code 163(c) permits homeowners living on a leased parcel to deduct their ground rent payments if (a) the ground lease is for at least 15 years, including renewal periods, (b) the lease is freely assignable to the buyer of your home, (c) the land owner's interest is primarily a security interest (like a mortgage) and (d) you have a current or future option to buy the land beneath your residence. If you do not have an option to buy the land (such as in a mobile home park), your ground rent payments do not qualify as tax-deductible itemized interest.

10. **Deduct moving costs if you changed job and residence locations.**

Whether you rent or own your home, if you changed both your job and residence locations, your moving costs might be tax-deductible. If you made a major cross-country move, the result can be a significant savings of income tax dollars. To qualify, the distance from your old home to your new job site must be at least 50 miles further from your old home than was your old job location.

EXAMPLE
➲

For example, suppose your old home was five miles from your old job site. That means your new job location must be at least 55 miles (5 plus 50) from your old home to qualify for moving costs deduction. The distance to your new job location from your new residence is irrelevant.

If you passed the distance test, the second qualification requires you to be employed at least 39 weeks during the next 52 weeks in the vicinity of your new job location; you need not work for the same employer and either spouse can qualify. If you are self-employed, however, you must work at least 78 weeks during the next 104 weeks in the vicinity of your new job site.

Non-Deductible Home Purchase Costs

Every year millions of new and resale houses, condos and town homes change ownership. If you're among those home buyers and sellers, you probably paid non-deductible closing costs such as transfer tax, recording fees, escrow attorney or title costs and other non-deductible expenses.

If you were a buyer, add these costs to your home's purchase price *adjusted cost basis.* If you were a seller, these sales expenses should be subtracted from the gross sales price to arrive at your adjusted sales price.

The home buyer's adjusted costs basis is the sum of the home's purchase price, plus acquisition expenses that were not deductible in the year of purchase. The cost of any capital improvements added during ownership should be added to this adjusted cost basis. Be sure to save improvement cost receipts.

The home seller's adjusted sales price is the gross sales price minus selling expenses, such as transfer fees, recording charges, and real estate sales commission.

To determine the home's capital gain profit, subtract the adjusted cost basis from the adjusted sales price. If you qualify for the Internal Revenue Code 121 principal residence sale tax exemption, up to $250,000 or $500,000 of your home sale profit will be tax-free.

For more details on these and other homeowner and real estate investor tax benefits, please consult your tax adviser.

Do It Yourself:
Secrets to a Successful Move

If the cost of hiring professionals to move you from point A to point B is out of the question, take heart. With a little organization and advance planning, you can do it yourself!

A Moving Timeline

ST
Ɔ

Six to eight weeks prior:

- Start looking for boxes in a variety of shapes and sizes. Free boxes from supermarkets or liquor stores are fine, but make sure they are clean and sturdy. Boxes with tops and handles are best.

- Collect more boxes than you think you may need. You can buy boxes from a moving company, truck rental agency or packing store, but they can be expensive. Always try to keep boxes to 50 pounds or less and reinforce box bottoms with at least one strip of packing tape.

- Save newspapers and other materials to pack belongings inside boxes.

- If you're planning a long-distance move, consider freight companies as an alternative to driving a rental truck. You might find that the costs are lower than you think.

Five weeks prior:

- Pare down clothes and household items by planning a garage sale. You'll have less to pack and the extra money you'll earn can be put toward the little expenses that quickly add up when you're moving.

- If you're making an out-of-state move, check your insurance policies (auto, health and homeowner's) to see if the move will affect your services. Since homeowner's policies rarely offer full coverage for moving, inquire if you can purchase an additional policy.
- Make arrangements for enrollments in new schools.

Four weeks prior:

- Begin packing several cartons each day. Work room by room and as you go through cabinets, closets and drawers separate items to be sold at the garage sale and those that will be given to charity.
- Call utility companies to disconnect services at your current address and give new utility companies a date to connect services at your new residence. Additionally, arrange for last service dates (i.e. newspaper, gardener, housekeeping, etc.); either settle accounts or supply vendors with your new address to bill.
- Notify post office about your upcoming change of address. Send change of address notices to family and friends and remember to mark address changes on the return portion of bills.
- Seek advice from your veterinarian about moving animals. If necessary, purchase pet carriers or crates. Remember that if you plan to fly to your new home, your animals will need special papers. Check with the airlines for their requirements and remember that in the western states, most of them will not transport animals in the summer.

One to two weeks prior:

- Have vehicles inspected and tuned up if you're moving long distance.
- Make an effort to use up fresh and frozen foods in your refrigerator and freezer. When supplies are depleted, defrost and clean refrigerator thoroughly. Put some baking soda or coffee grounds in a sock and place it inside to keep the interior smelling fresh.
- Empty barbecue grills' propane tanks, drain gasoline and oil from power equipment and properly purge water from hoses.

- Pack computers, stereo equipment, televisions and other electronics and appliances; whenever possible, use their original boxes.

Moving day:
- Walk through each room, checking closets and built-ins to make sure nothing will be left behind. Verify everything has been cleared out from attics, garages and tool sheds.

Packing Essentials Checklist

✓ Strong boxes (some wardrobe boxes are recommended)

✓ Plastic footlockers (for fragile items)

✓ Bubble wrap

✓ Large plastic bags or shrink-wrap to protect belongings

✓ Moving pads and/or blankets and quilts for padding furniture

✓ Clothesline or rope

✓ Scissors or pocketknife (to cut rope)

✓ Dolly/hand truck

✓ Broad-tip markers to label boxes

✓ Colored stickers for room assignments

✓ Rolls of packing tape (2-inch wide and a tape dispenser is recommended)

✓ Tissue and ink-free packing paper

Packing Pointers

- Pack room by room keeping similar items together; it's best not to mix items from different rooms in the same box.
- Place record albums and CDs vertically in boxes; avoid stacking them flat.
- Prevent small items from being lost or mistakenly discarded with the packing materials by wrapping them in brightly colored tissue paper.
- Use smaller boxes for books and larger boxes for lighter items; always place heavier contents in the bottom of the box and lighter items on top.
- Use linens and towels to pad boxes of fragile items. Make sure these boxes are clearly marked to avoid breakage.

- On the top and front of each carton, write a description of the contents and note which room it came from. Apply different colored stickers on each box, then at your new house post a matching sticker (or balloons with the corresponding colors) outside the room where you want the color-coded box to go.

- Whenever possible, detach legs from furniture and place all bolts/screws in a plastic bag and tape it to the item it was removed from. Also, remove bulbs before packing lamps. (Use an oversized, well-cushioned box for packing lamp shades.)

- Secure drawers of furniture from opening during transit.

- Put together a box of necessities and label it "Essentials." This box should include: toiletries, towels, sheets, necessary medications, toilet paper, flashlights, pocketknife, hammer, nails, screwdrivers, tape measure, masking tape, light bulbs, paper plates and cups, plastic utensils, paper towels and trash bags.

- Keep important and irreplaceable items close by. Never leave medical records, financial or legal papers such as bank checks, insurance policies, stock certificates, passports and valuables (jewelry, rare coins, stamp collections, etc.) unattended.

 Beware of hazardous materials that should not be packed, such as flammables (paint, varnish and thinners), some cleaning fluids and detergents, aerosol cans, gasoline, kerosene, ammunition, explosives and corrosives.

Remember to...

- Take along your current phone book. You may need to contact businesses or residents in your former hometown.

- Avoid scorching the leaves of houseplants when transporting them by car to your new home. Don't lean them against windows.

- Keep pets calm on moving day. Arrange for a friend to watch them until you're ready to leave.

- Resist plugging in computers right away. They need time to "acclimate" to the temperature of their new surroundings.

Loading & Unloading

- Load heavy items on bottom of truck or trailer, lighter items on top.

- Make the most of your space; pack high and tight to prevent rubbing or shifting during transit.

- Use rope whenever possible to make things extra stable.

- Keep children's items from being loaded too soon so little ones don't have to wait for their belongings.

- Unpack fragile items over the box you are removing them from so if you drop an item it will land on packing material and reduce the likelihood of breakage.

Resources

Sample Forms

CALIFORNIA ASSOCIATION OF REALTORS®

CALIFORNIA
RESIDENTIAL PURCHASE AGREEMENT
AND JOINT ESCROW INSTRUCTIONS
For Use With Single Family Residential Property — Attached or Detached
(C.A.R. Form RPA-CA, Revised 10/02)

Date _____ at _____, California.
1. **OFFER:**
   A. **THIS IS AN OFFER FROM** _____ ("Buyer").
   B. **THE REAL PROPERTY TO BE ACQUIRED** is described as _____
      _____, Assessor's Parcel No. _____, situated in
      _____, County of _____, California, ("Property").
   C. **THE PURCHASE PRICE** offered is _____
      _____ Dollars $ _____.
   D. **CLOSE OF ESCROW** shall occur on _____ (date)(or ☐ _____ **Days** After Acceptance).
2. **FINANCE TERMS:** Obtaining the loans below **is a contingency** of this Agreement unless: **(i)** either 2K or 2L is checked below; or **(ii)** otherwise agreed in writing. Buyer shall act diligently and in good faith to obtain the designated loans. Obtaining deposit, down payment and closing costs **is not a contingency.** Buyer represents that funds will be good when deposited with Escrow Holder.
   A. **INITIAL DEPOSIT:** Buyer has given a deposit in the amount of .... $ _____
      to the agent submitting the offer (or to ☐ _____), by personal check
      (or ☐ _____), made payable to _____,
      which shall be held uncashed until Acceptance and then deposited within **3** business days after
      Acceptance (or ☐ _____), with
      Escrow Holder, (or ☐ into Broker's trust account).
   B. **INCREASED DEPOSIT:** Buyer shall deposit with Escrow Holder an increased deposit in the amount of . . . . $ _____
      within ____ **Days** After Acceptance, or ☐ _____.
   C. **FIRST LOAN IN THE AMOUNT OF** .... $ _____
      (1) NEW First Deed of Trust in favor of lender, encumbering the Property, securing a note payable at
      maximum interest of _____% fixed rate, or _____% initial adjustable rate with a maximum
      interest rate of _____%, balance due in _____ years, amortized over _____ years. Buyer
      shall pay loan fees/points not to exceed _____. (These terms apply whether the designated loan
      is conventional, FHA or VA.)
      (2) ☐ FHA ☐ VA: (The following terms only apply to the FHA or VA loan that is checked.)
      Seller shall pay _____% discount points. Seller shall pay other fees not allowed to be paid by
      Buyer, ☐ not to exceed $ _____. Seller shall pay the cost of lender required Repairs
      (including those for wood destroying pest) not otherwise provided for in this Agreement, ☐ not to
      exceed $ _____. (Actual loan amount may increase if mortgage insurance premiums,
      funding fees or closing costs are financed.)
   D. **ADDITIONAL FINANCING TERMS:** ☐ Seller financing, ...R. Form SF_ ___ secondary financing, ... $ _____
      (C.A.R. Form PAA, paragraph 4A); ☐ assumed fin_ _ _ g (C.A.R. F_ __ A, __ragraph 4B)
      _____
      _____
   E. **BALANCE OF PURCHASE PRICE** (not including costs of obtaining loans and other closing costs) in the amount of . . . $ _____
      to be deposited with Escrow Holder within sufficient time to close escrow.
   F. **PURCHASE PRICE (TOTAL):** .... $ _____
   G. **LOAN APPLICATIONS:** Within **7** (or _____) **Days** After Acceptance, Buyer shall provide Seller a letter from lender or
      mortgage loan broker stating that, based on a review of Buyer's written application and credit report, Buyer is prequalified or
      preapproved for the NEW loan specified in 2C above.
   H. **VERIFICATION OF DOWN PAYMENT AND CLOSING COSTS:** Buyer (or Buyer's lender or loan broker pursuant to 2G) shall, within
      7 (or ☐ _____) **Days** After Acceptance, provide Seller written verification of Buyer's down payment and closing costs.
   I. **LOAN CONTINGENCY REMOVAL:** (i) Within **17** (or ☐ _____) **Days** After Acceptance, Buyer shall, as specified in paragraph
      14, remove the loan contingency or cancel this Agreement; **OR** (ii) (if checked) ☐ the loan contingency shall remain in effect
      until the designated loans are funded.
   J. **APPRAISAL CONTINGENCY AND REMOVAL:** This Agreement is (**OR**, if checked, ☐ is NOT) contingent upon the Property
      appraising at no less than the specified purchase price. If there is a loan contingency, at the time the loan contingency is
      removed (or, if checked, ☐ within **17** (or _____) **Days** After Acceptance), Buyer shall, as specified in paragraph
      14B(3), remove the appraisal contingency or cancel this Agreement. If there is no loan contingency, Buyer shall, as specified in paragraph
      14B(3), remove the appraisal contingency within **17** (or _____) **Days** After Acceptance.
   K. ☐ **NO LOAN CONTINGENCY** (If checked): Obtaining any loan in paragraphs 2C, 2D or elsewhere in this Agreement is NOT
      a contingency of this Agreement. If Buyer does not obtain the loan and as a result Buyer does not purchase the Property, Seller
      may be entitled to Buyer's deposit or other legal remedies.
   L. ☐ **ALL CASH OFFER** (If checked): No loan is needed to purchase the Property. Buyer shall, within **7** (or ☐ _____) **Days** After Acceptance,
      provide Seller written verification of sufficient funds to close this transaction.
3. **CLOSING AND OCCUPANCY:**
   A. Buyer intends (or ☐ does not intend) to occupy the Property as Buyer's primary residence.
   B. **Seller-occupied or vacant property:** Occupancy shall be delivered to Buyer at _____ AM/PM, ☐ on the date of Close Of
      Escrow; ☐ on _____; or ☐ no later than _____ **Days** After Close Of Escrow. (C.A.R. Form PAA, paragraph 2.) If
      transfer of title and occupancy do not occur at the same time, Buyer and Seller are advised to: **(i)** enter into a written occupancy
      agreement; and **(ii)** consult with their insurance and legal advisors.

RPA-CA REVISED 10/02 (PAGE 1 OF 8) Print Date

Buyer's Initials (_____)(_____)
Seller's Initials (_____)(_____)

Reviewed by _____ Date _____

EQUAL HOUSING OPPORTUNITY

CALIFORNIA RESIDENTIAL PURCHASE AGREEMENT (RPA-CA PAGE 1 OF 8)

Property Address: _____ Date: _____

C. **Tenant-occupied property: (i) Property shall be vacant** at least 5 **(or** ☐ _____ **) Days** Prior to Close Of Escrow, unless otherwise agreed in writing. **Note to Seller: If you are unable to deliver Property vacant in accordance with rent control and other applicable Law, you may be in breach of this Agreement.**

OR **(ii)** (if checked) ☐ **Tenant to remain in possession.** The attached addendum is incorporated into this Agreement (C.A.R. Form PAA, paragraph 3.);

OR **(iii)** (if checked) ☐ **This Agreement is contingent** upon Buyer and Seller entering into a written agreement regarding occupancy of the Property within the time specified in paragraph 14B(1). If no written agreement is reached within this time, either Buyer or Seller may cancel this Agreement in writing.

D. At Close Of Escrow, Seller assigns to Buyer any assignable warranty rights for items included in the sale and shall provide any available Copies of such warranties. Brokers cannot and will not determine the assignability of any warranties.

E. At Close Of Escrow, unless otherwise agreed in writing, Seller shall provide keys and/or means to operate all locks, mailboxes, security systems, alarms and garage door openers. If Property is a condominium or located in a common interest subdivision, Buyer may be required to pay a deposit to the Homeowners' Association ("HOA") to obtain keys to accessible HOA facilities.

4. **ALLOCATION OF COSTS** (If checked): Unless otherwise specified here, this paragraph only determines who is to pay for the report, inspection, test or service mentioned. If not specified here or elsewhere in this Agreement, the determination of who is to pay for any work recommended or identified by any such report, inspection, test or service shall be by the method specified in paragraph 14B(2).

A. **WOOD DESTROYING PEST INSPECTION:**
   (1) ☐ Buyer ☐ Seller shall pay for an inspection and report for wood destroying pests and organisms ("Report") which shall be prepared by _____, a registered structural pest control company. The Report shall cover the accessible areas of the main building and attached structures and, if checked: ☐ detached garages and carports, ☐ detached decks, ☐ the following other structures or areas _____. The Report shall not include roof coverings. If Property is a condominium or located in a common interest subdivision, the Report shall include only the separate interest and any exclusive-use areas being transferred and shall not include common areas, unless otherwise agreed. Water tests of shower pans on upper level units may not be performed without consent of the owners of property below the shower.

OR (2) ☐ **(If checked)** The attached addendum (C.A.R. Form WPA) regarding wood destroying pest inspection and allocation of cost is incorporated into this Agreement.

B. **OTHER INSPECTIONS AND REPORTS:**
   (1) ☐ Buyer ☐ Seller shall pay to have septic or private sewage disposal systems inspected _____.
   (2) ☐ Buyer ☐ Seller shall pay to have domestic wells tested for water potability and productivity _____.
   (3) ☐ Buyer ☐ Seller shall pay for a natural hazard zone disclosure report prepared by _____.
   (4) ☐ Buyer ☐ Seller shall pay for the following inspection or report _____.
   (5) ☐ Buyer ☐ Seller shall pay for the following inspection or report _____.

C. **GOVERNMENT REQUIREMENTS AND RETROFIT:**
   (1) ☐ Buyer ☐ Seller shall pay for smoke detector installation and/or water heater bracing, if required by Law. Prior to Close Of Escrow, Seller shall provide Buyer a written statement of compliance in accordance with state and local Law, unless exempt.
   (2) ☐ Buyer ☐ Seller shall pay the cost of compliance with any other minimum mandatory government retrofit standards, inspections and reports if required as a condition of closing escrow under any Law. _____.

D. **ESCROW AND TITLE:**
   (1) ☐ Buyer ☐ Seller shall pay escrow fee _____.
   Escrow Holder shall be _____.
   (2) ☐ Buyer ☐ Seller shall pay for **owner's** title insurance policy specified in paragraph 12E _____.
   Owner's title policy to be issued by _____.
   (Buyer shall pay for any title insurance policy insuring Buyer's **lender**, unless otherwise agreed in writing.)

E. **OTHER COSTS:**
   (1) ☐ Buyer ☐ Seller shall pay County transfer tax or transfer fee _____.
   (2) ☐ Buyer ☐ Seller shall pay City transfer tax or transfer fee _____.
   (3) ☐ Buyer ☐ Seller shall pay HOA transfer fee _____.
   (4) ☐ Buyer ☐ Seller shall pay HOA document preparation fees _____.
   (5) ☐ Buyer ☐ Seller shall pay the cost, not to exceed $ _____, of a one-year home warranty plan, issued by _____ with the following optional coverage: _____.
   (6) ☐ Buyer ☐ Seller shall pay for _____.
   (7) ☐ Buyer ☐ Seller shall pay for _____.

5. **STATUTORY DISCLOSURES (INCLUDING LEAD-BASED PAINT HAZARD DISCLOSURES) AND CANCELLATION RIGHTS:**
A. (1) Seller shall, within the time specified in paragraph 14A, deliver to Buyer, if required by Law: **(i)** Federal Lead-Based Paint Disclosures and pamphlet ("Lead Disclosures"); and **(ii)** disclosures or notices required by sections 1102 et. seq. and 1103 et. seq. of the California Civil Code ("Statutory Disclosures"). Statutory Disclosures include, but are not limited to, a Real Estate Transfer Disclosure Statement ("TDS"), Natural Hazard Disclosure Statement ("NHD"), notice or actual knowledge of release of illegal controlled substance, notice of special tax and/or assessments (or, if allowed, substantially equivalent notice regarding the Mello-Roos Community Facilities Act and Improvement Bond Act of 1915) and, if Seller has actual knowledge, an industrial use and military ordnance location disclosure (C.A.R. Form SSD).
   (2) Buyer shall, within the time specified in paragraph 14B(1), return Signed Copies of the Statutory and Lead Disclosures to Seller.
   (3) In the event Seller, prior to Close Of Escrow, becomes aware of adverse conditions materially affecting the Property, or any material inaccuracy in disclosures, information or representations previously provided to Buyer of which Buyer is otherwise unaware, Seller shall promptly provide a subsequent or amended disclosure or notice, in writing, covering those items. **However, a subsequent or amended disclosure shall not be required for conditions and material inaccuracies disclosed in reports ordered and paid for by Buyer.**

Buyer's Initials (_____)(_____)
Seller's Initials (_____)(_____)

RPA-CA REVISED 10/02 (PAGE 2 OF 8)

Reviewed by _____ Date _____

EQUAL HOUSING OPPORTUNITY

CALIFORNIA RESIDENTIAL PURCHASE AGREEMENT (RPA-CA PAGE 2 OF 8)

Residential Purchase Agreement and Joint Escrow Instructions

Property Address: _____ Date: _____

(4) If any disclosure or notice specified in 5A(1), or subsequent or amended disclosure or notice is delivered to Buyer after the offer is Signed, Buyer shall have the right to cancel this Agreement within **3 Days** After delivery in person, or **5 Days** After delivery by deposit in the mail, by giving written notice of cancellation to Seller or Seller's agent. (Lead Disclosures sent by mail must be sent certified mail or better.)

(5) **Note to Buyer and Seller: Waiver of Statutory and Lead Disclosures is prohibited by Law.**

B. **NATURAL AND ENVIRONMENTAL HAZARDS:** Within the time specified in paragraph 14A, Seller shall, if required by Law: **(i)** deliver to Buyer earthquake guides (and questionnaire) and environmental hazards booklet; **(ii)** even if exempt from the obligation to provide a NHD, disclose if the Property is located in a Special Flood Hazard Area; Potential Flooding (Inundation) Area; Very High Fire Hazard Zone; State Fire Responsibility Area; Earthquake Fault Zone; Seismic Hazard Zone; and **(iii)** disclose any other zone as required by Law and provide any other information required for those zones.

C. **DATA BASE DISCLOSURE:** NOTICE: The California Department of Justice, sheriff's departments, police departments serving jurisdictions of 200,000 or more and many other local law enforcement authorities maintain for public access a data base of the locations of persons required to register pursuant to paragraph (1) of subdivision (a) of Section 290.4 of the Penal Code. The data base is updated on a quarterly basis and a source of information about the presence of these individuals in any neighborhood. The Department of Justice also maintains a Sex Offender Identification Line through which inquiries about individuals may be made. This is a "900" telephone service. Callers must have specific information about individuals they are checking. Information regarding neighborhoods is not available through the "900" telephone service.

6. **CONDOMINIUM/PLANNED UNIT DEVELOPMENT DISCLOSURES:**

   A. **SELLER HAS: 7 (or ☐ _____) Days** After Acceptance to disclose to Buyer whether the Property is a condominium, or is located in a planned unit development or other common interest subdivision (C.A.R. Form SSD).

   B. If the Property is a condominium or is located in a planned unit development or other common interest subdivision, Seller has **3 (or ☐ _____) Days** After Acceptance to request from the HOA (C.A.R. Form HOA): **(i)** Copies of any documents required by Law; **(ii)** disclosure of any pending or anticipated claim or litigation by or against the HOA; **(iii)** a statement containing the location and number of designated parking and storage spaces; **(iv)** Copies of the most recent 12 months of HOA minutes for regular and special meetings; and **(v)** the names and contact information of all HOAs governing the Property (collectively, "CI Disclosures"). Seller shall itemize and deliver to Buyer all CI Disclosures received from the HOA and any CI Disclosures in Seller's possession. Buyer's approval of CI Disclosures is a contingency of this Agreement as specified in paragraph 14B(3).

7. **CONDITIONS AFFECTING PROPERTY:**

   A. Unless otherwise agreed: **(i) the Property is sold (a) in its PRESENT physical condition as of the date of Acceptance and (b) subject to Buyer's Investigation rights; (ii)** the Property, including pool, spa, landscaping and grounds, is to be maintained in substantially the same condition as on the date of Acceptance; and **(iii)** all debris and personal property not included in the sale shall be removed by Close Of Escrow.

   B. **SELLER SHALL,** within the time specified in paragraph 14A, DISCLOSE KNOWN MATERIAL FACTS AND DEFECTS affecting the Property, including known insurance claims within the past five years, AND MAKE OTHER DISCLOSURES REQUIRED BY LAW (C.A.R. Form SSD).

   C. **NOTE TO BUYER: You are strongly advised to conduct investigations of the entire Property in order to determine its present condition since Seller may not be aware of all defects affecting the Property or other factors that you consider important. Property improvements may not be built according to code, in compliance with current Law, or have had permits issued.**

   D. **NOTE TO SELLER: Buyer has the right to inspect the Property and, as specified in paragraph 14B, based upon information discovered in those inspections: (i) cancel this Agreement; or (ii) request that you make Repairs or take other action.**

8. **ITEMS INCLUDED AND EXCLUDED:**

   A. **NOTE TO BUYER AND SELLER:** Items listed as included or excluded in the MLS, flyers or marketing materials are **not** included in the purchase price or excluded from the sale unless specified in 8B or C.

   B. **ITEMS INCLUDED IN SALE:**

   (1) All EXISTING fixtures and fittings that are attached to the Property;

   (2) Existing electrical, mechanical, lighting, plumbing and heating fixtures, ceiling fans, fireplace inserts, gas logs and grates, solar systems, built-in appliances, window and door screens, awnings, shutters, window coverings, attached floor coverings, television antennas, satellite dishes, private integrated telephone systems, air coolers/conditioners, pool/spa equipment, garage door openers/remote controls, mailbox, in-ground landscaping, trees/shrubs, water softeners, water purifiers, security systems/alarms; and

   (3) The following items: _____
   _____.

   (4) Seller represents that all items included in the purchase price, unless otherwise specified, are owned by Seller.

   (5) All items included shall be transferred free of liens and without Seller warranty.

   C. **ITEMS EXCLUDED FROM SALE:** _____
   _____.

9. **BUYER'S INVESTIGATION OF PROPERTY AND MATTERS AFFECTING PROPERTY:**

   A. Buyer's acceptance of the condition of, and any other matter affecting the Property, is a contingency of this Agreement as specified in this paragraph and paragraph 14B. Within the time specified in paragraph 14B(1), Buyer shall have the right, at Buyer's expense unless otherwise agreed, to conduct inspections, investigations, tests, surveys and other studies ("Buyer Investigations"), including, but not limited to, the right to: **(i)** inspect for lead-based paint and other lead-based paint hazards; **(ii)** inspect for wood destroying pests and organisms; **(iii)** review the registered sex offender database; **(iv)** confirm the insurability of Buyer and the Property; and **(v)** satisfy Buyer as to any matter specified in the attached Buyer's Inspection Advisory (C.A.R. Form BIA). Without Seller's prior written consent, Buyer shall neither make nor cause to be made: **(i)** invasive or destructive Buyer Investigations; or **(ii)** inspections by any governmental building or zoning inspector or government employee, unless required by Law.

   B. Buyer shall complete Buyer Investigations, as specified in paragraph 14B, remove the contingency or cancel this Agreement. Buyer shall give Seller, at no cost, complete Copies of all Buyer Investigation reports obtained by Buyer. Seller shall make the Property available for all Buyer Investigations. Seller shall have water, gas, electricity and all operable pilot lights on for Buyer's Investigations and through the date possession is made available to Buyer.

Buyer's Initials (_____)(_____)
Seller's Initials (_____)(_____)

Reviewed by _____ Date _____

EQUAL HOUSING OPPORTUNITY

CALIFORNIA RESIDENTIAL PURCHASE AGREEMENT (RPA-CA PAGE 3 OF 8)

Residential Purchase Agreement and Joint Escrow Instructions

Property Address: _____ Date: _____

10. **REPAIRS:** Repairs shall be completed prior to final verification of condition unless otherwise agreed in writing. Repairs to be performed at Seller's expense may be performed by Seller or through others, provided that the work complies with applicable Law, including governmental permit, inspection and approval requirements. Repairs shall be performed in a good, skillful manner with materials of quality and appearance comparable to existing materials. It is understood that exact restoration of appearance or cosmetic items following all Repairs may not be possible. Seller shall: **(i)** obtain receipts for Repairs performed by others; **(ii)** prepare a written statement indicating the Repairs performed by Seller and the date of such Repairs; and **(iii)** provide Copies of receipts and statements to Buyer prior to final verification of condition.

11. **BUYER INDEMNITY AND SELLER PROTECTION FOR ENTRY UPON PROPERTY:** Buyer shall: **(i)** keep the Property free and clear of liens; **(ii)** Repair all damage arising from Buyer Investigations; and **(iii)** indemnify and hold Seller harmless from all resulting liability, claims, demands, damages and costs. Buyer shall carry, or Buyer shall require anyone acting on Buyer's behalf to carry, policies of liability, workers' compensation and other applicable insurance, defending and protecting Seller from liability for any injuries to persons or property occurring during any Buyer Investigations or work done on the Property at Buyer's direction prior to Close Of Escrow. Seller is advised that certain protections may be afforded Seller by recording a "Notice of Non-responsibility" (C.A.R. Form NNR) for Buyer Investigations and work done on the Property at Buyer's direction. Buyer's obligations under this paragraph shall survive the termination of this Agreement.

12. **TITLE AND VESTING:**
   A. Within the time specified in paragraph 14, Buyer shall be provided a current preliminary (title) report, which is only an offer by the title insurer to issue a policy of title insurance and may not contain every item affecting title. Buyer's review of the preliminary report and any other matters which may affect title are a contingency of this Agreement as specified in paragraph 14B.
   B. Title is taken in its present condition subject to all encumbrances, easements, covenants, conditions, restrictions, rights and other matters, whether of record or not, as of the date of Acceptance except: **(i)** monetary liens of record unless Buyer is assuming those obligations or taking the Property subject to those obligations; and **(ii)** those matters which Seller has agreed to remove in writing.
   C. Within the time specified in paragraph 14A, Seller has a duty to disclose to Buyer all matters known to Seller affecting title, whether of record or not.
   D. At Close Of Escrow, Buyer shall receive a grant deed conveying title (or, for stock cooperative or long-term lease, an assignment of stock certificate or of Seller's leasehold interest), including oil, mineral and water rights if currently owned by Seller. Title shall vest as designated in Buyer's supplemental escrow instructions. THE MANNER OF TAKING TITLE MAY HAVE SIGNIFICANT LEGAL AND TAX CONSEQUENCES. CONSULT AN APPROPRIATE PROFESSIONAL.
   E. Buyer shall receive a CLTA/ALTA Homeowner's Policy of Title Insurance. A title company, at Buyer's request, can provide information about the availability, desirability, coverage, and cost of various title insurance coverages and endorsements. If Buyer desires title coverage other than that required by this paragraph, Buyer shall instruct Escrow Holder in writing and pay any increase in cost.

13. **SALE OF BUYER'S PROPERTY:**
   A. This Agreement is NOT contingent upon the sale of any property owned by Buyer.
   OR B. ☐ (If checked): The attached addendum (C.A.R. Form COP) regarding the contingency for the sale of property owned by Buyer is incorporated into this Agreement.

14. **TIME PERIODS; REMOVAL OF CONTINGENCIES; CANCELLATION RIGHTS: The following time periods may only be extended, altered, modified or changed by mutual written agreement. Any removal of contingencies or cancellation under this paragraph must be in writing (C.A.R. Form CR).**
   A. **SELLER HAS: 7 (or ☐ _____) Days** After Acceptance to deliver to Buyer all reports, disclosures and information for which Seller is responsible under paragraphs 4, 5A and B, 6A, 7B and 12.
   B. **(1) BUYER HAS: 17 (or ☐ _____) Days** After Acceptance, unless otherwise agreed in writing, to:
      (i) complete all Buyer Investigations; approve all disclosures, reports and other applicable information, which Buyer receives from Seller; and approve all matters affecting the Property (including lead-based paint and lead-based paint hazards as well as other information specified in paragraph 5 and insurability of Buyer and the Property); and
      (ii) return to Seller Signed Copies of Statutory and Lead Disclosures delivered by Seller in accordance with paragraph 5A.
      (2) Within the time specified in 14B(1), Buyer may request that Seller make repairs or take any other action regarding the Property (C.A.R. Form RR). Seller has no obligation to agree to or respond to Buyer's requests.
      (3) By the end of the time specified in 14B(1) (or 2I for loan contingency or 2J for appraisal contingency), Buyer shall, in writing, remove the applicable contingency (C.A.R. Form CR) or cancel this Agreement. However, if **(i)** government-mandated inspections/ reports required as a condition of closing; or **(ii)** Common Interest Disclosures pursuant to paragraph 6B are not made within the time specified in 14A, then Buyer has **5 (or ☐ _____) Days** After receipt of any such items, or the time specified in 14B(1), whichever is later, to remove the applicable contingency or cancel this Agreement in writing.
   C. **CONTINUATION OF CONTINGENCY OR CONTRACTUAL OBLIGATION; SELLER RIGHT TO CANCEL:**
      (1) Seller right to Cancel; Buyer Contingencies: Seller, after first giving Buyer a Notice to Buyer to Perform (as specified below), may cancel this Agreement in writing and authorize return of Buyer's deposit if, by the time specified in this Agreement, Buyer does not remove in writing the applicable contingency or cancel this Agreement. Once all contingencies have been removed, failure of either Buyer or Seller to close escrow on time may be a breach of this Agreement.
      (2) Continuation of Contingency: Even after the expiration of the time specified in 14B, Buyer retains the right to make requests to Seller, remove in writing the applicable contingency or cancel this Agreement until Seller cancels pursuant to 14C(1). Once Seller receives Buyer's written removal of all contingencies, Seller may not cancel this Agreement pursuant to 14C(1).
      (3) Seller right to Cancel; Buyer Contract Obligations: Seller, after first giving Buyer a Notice to Buyer to Perform (as specified below), may cancel this Agreement in writing and authorize return of Buyer's deposit for any of the following reasons: **(i)** if Buyer fails to deposit funds as required by 2A or 2B; **(ii)** if the funds deposited pursuant to 2A or 2B are not good when deposited; **(iii)** if Buyer fails to provide a letter as required by 2G; **(iv)** if Buyer fails to provide verification as required by 2H or 2L; **(v)** if Seller reasonably disapproves of the verification provided by 2H or 2L; **(vi)** if Buyer fails to return Statutory and Lead Disclosures as required by paragraph 5A(2); or **(vii)** if Buyer fails to sign or initial a separate liquidated damage form for an increased deposit as required by paragraph 16. **Seller is not required to give Buyer a Notice to Perform regarding Close of Escrow.**
      (4) Notice To Buyer To Perform: The Notice to Buyer to Perform (C.A.R. Form NBP) shall: **(i)** be in writing; **(ii)** be signed by Seller; and **(iii)** give Buyer at least **24 (or ☐ _____)** hours (or until the time specified in the applicable paragraph, whichever occurs last) to take the applicable action. A Notice to Buyer to Perform may not be given any earlier than **2 Days** Prior to the expiration of the applicable time for Buyer to remove a contingency or cancel this Agreement or meet a 14C(3) obligation.

Buyer's Initials (_____)(_____)
Seller's Initials (_____)(_____)

RPA-CA REVISED 10/02 (PAGE 4 OF 8)

Reviewed by _____ Date _____

EQUAL HOUSING OPPORTUNITY

CALIFORNIA RESIDENTIAL PURCHASE AGREEMENT (RPA-CA PAGE 4 OF 8)

Residential Purchase Agreement and Joint Escrow Instructions

Property Address: _____ Date: _____

D. **EFFECT OF BUYER'S REMOVAL OF CONTINGENCIES :** If Buyer removes, in writing, any contingency or cancellation rights, unless otherwise specified in a separate written agreement between Buyer and Seller, Buyer shall conclusively be deemed to have: **(i)** completed all Buyer Investigations, and review of reports and other applicable information and disclosures pertaining to that contingency or cancellation right; **(ii)** elected to proceed with the transaction; and **(iii)** assumed all liability, responsibility and expense for Repairs or corrections pertaining to that contingency or cancellation right, or for inability to obtain financing.

E. **EFFECT OF CANCELLATION ON DEPOSITS:** If Buyer or Seller gives written notice of cancellation pursuant to rights duly exercised under the terms of this Agreement, Buyer and Seller agree to Sign mutual instructions to cancel the sale and escrow and release deposits to the party entitled to the funds, less fees and costs incurred by that party. Fees and costs may be payable to service providers and vendors for services and products provided during escrow. **Release of funds will require mutual Signed release instructions from Buyer and Seller, judicial decision or arbitration award. A party may be subject to a civil penalty of up to $1,000 for refusal to sign such instructions if no good faith dispute exists as to who is entitled to the deposited funds** (Civil Code §1057.3).

15. **FINAL VERIFICATION OF CONDITION:** Buyer shall have the right to make a final inspection of the Property within **5 (or _____) Days** Prior to Close Of Escrow, NOT AS A CONTINGENCY OF THE SALE, but solely to confirm: **(i)** the Property is maintained pursuant to paragraph 7A; **(ii)** Repairs have been completed as agreed; and **(iii)** Seller has complied with Seller's other obligations under this Agreement.

16. **LIQUIDATED DAMAGES: If Buyer fails to complete this purchase because of Buyer's default, Seller shall retain, as liquidated damages, the deposit actually paid. If the Property is a dwelling with no more than four units, one of which Buyer intends to occupy, then the amount retained shall be no more than 3% of the purchase price. Any excess shall be returned to Buyer. Release of funds will require mutual, Signed release instructions from both Buyer and Seller, judicial decision or arbitration award.**
BUYER AND SELLER SHALL SIGN A SEPARATE LIQUIDATED DAMAGES PROVISION FOR ANY INCREASED DEPOSIT. (C.A.R. FORM RID)

Buyer's Initials _____/_____	Seller's Initials _____/_____

17. **DISPUTE RESOLUTION:**

A. **MEDIATION:** Buyer and Seller agree to mediate any dispute or claim arising between them out of this Agreement, or any resulting transaction, before resorting to arbitration or court action. Paragraphs 17B(2) and (3) below apply whether or not the Arbitration provision is initialed. Mediation fees, if any, shall be divided equally among the parties involved. If, for any dispute or claim to which this paragraph applies, any party commences an action without first attempting to resolve the matter through mediation, or refuses to mediate after a request has been made, then that party shall not be entitled to recover attorney fees, even if they would otherwise be available to that party in any such action. THIS MEDIATION PROVISION APPLIES WHETHER OR NOT THE ARBITRATION PROVISION IS INITIALED.

B. **ARBITRATION OF DISPUTES: (1) Buyer and Seller agree that any dispute or claim in Law or equity arising between them out of this Agreement or any resulting transaction, which is not settled through mediation, shall be decided by neutral, binding arbitration, including and subject to paragraphs 17B(2) and (3) below. The arbitrator shall be a retired judge or justice, or an attorney with at least 5 years of residential real estate Law experience, unless the parties mutually agree to a different arbitrator, who shall render an award in accordance with substantive California Law. The parties shall have the right to discovery in accordance with California Code of Civil Procedure §1283.05. In all other respects, the arbitration shall be conducted in accordance with Title 9 of Part III of the California Code of Civil Procedure. Judgment upon the award of the arbitrator(s) may be entered into any court having jurisdiction. Interpretation of this agreement to arbitrate shall be governed by the Federal Arbitration Act.**
(2) EXCLUSIONS FROM MEDIATION AND ARBITRATION: The following matters are excluded from mediation and arbitration: (i) a judicial or non-judicial foreclosure or other action or proceeding to enforce a deed of trust, mortgage or installment land sale contract as defined in California Civil Code §2985; (ii) an unlawful detainer action; (iii) the filing or enforcement of a mechanic's lien; and (iv) any matter that is within the jurisdiction of a probate, small claims or bankruptcy court. The filing of a court action to enable the recording of a notice of pending action, for order of attachment, receivership, injunction, or other provisional remedies, shall not constitute a waiver of the mediation and arbitration provisions.
(3) BROKERS: Buyer and Seller agree to mediate and arbitrate disputes or claims involving either or both Brokers, consistent with 17A and B, provided either or both Brokers shall have agreed to such mediation or arbitration prior to, or within a reasonable time after, the dispute or claim is presented to Brokers. Any election by either or both Brokers to participate in mediation or arbitration shall not result in Brokers being deemed parties to the Agreement.
"NOTICE: BY INITIALING IN THE SPACE BELOW YOU ARE AGREEING TO HAVE ANY DISPUTE ARISING OUT OF THE MATTERS INCLUDED IN THE 'ARBITRATION OF DISPUTES' PROVISION DECIDED BY NEUTRAL ARBITRATION AS PROVIDED BY CALIFORNIA LAW AND YOU ARE GIVING UP ANY RIGHTS YOU MIGHT POSSESS TO HAVE THE DISPUTE LITIGATED IN A COURT OR JURY TRIAL. BY INITIALING IN THE SPACE BELOW YOU ARE GIVING UP YOUR JUDICIAL RIGHTS TO DISCOVERY AND APPEAL, UNLESS THOSE RIGHTS ARE SPECIFICALLY INCLUDED IN THE 'ARBITRATION OF DISPUTES' PROVISION. IF YOU REFUSE TO SUBMIT TO ARBITRATION AFTER AGREEING TO THIS PROVISION, YOU MAY BE COMPELLED TO ARBITRATE UNDER THE AUTHORITY OF THE CALIFORNIA CODE OF CIVIL PROCEDURE. YOUR AGREEMENT TO THIS ARBITRATION PROVISION IS VOLUNTARY."
"WE HAVE READ AND UNDERSTAND THE FOREGOING AND AGREE TO SUBMIT DISPUTES ARISING OUT OF THE MATTERS INCLUDED IN THE 'ARBITRATION OF DISPUTES' PROVISION TO NEUTRAL ARBITRATION."

Buyer's Initials _____/_____	Seller's Initials _____/_____

Buyer's Initials (_____)(_____)
Seller's Initials (_____)(_____)

Reviewed by _____ Date _____

EQUAL HOUSING OPPORTUNITY

CALIFORNIA RESIDENTIAL PURCHASE AGREEMENT (RPA-CA PAGE 5 OF 8)

Property Address: _____ Date: _____

18. **PRORATIONS OF PROPERTY TAXES AND OTHER ITEMS:** Unless otherwise agreed in writing, the following items shall be PAID CURRENT and prorated between Buyer and Seller as of Close Of Escrow: real property taxes and assessments, interest, rents, HOA regular, special, and emergency dues and assessments imposed prior to Close Of Escrow, premiums on insurance assumed by Buyer, payments on bonds and assessments assumed by Buyer, and payments on Mello-Roos and other Special Assessment District bonds and assessments that are now a lien. The following items shall be assumed by Buyer WITHOUT CREDIT toward the purchase price: prorated payments on Mello-Roos and other Special Assessment District bonds and assessments and HOA special assessments that are now a lien but not yet due. Property will be reassessed upon change of ownership. Any supplemental tax bills shall be paid as follows: **(i)** for periods after Close Of Escrow, by Buyer; and **(ii)** for periods prior to Close Of Escrow, by Seller. TAX BILLS ISSUED AFTER CLOSE OF ESCROW SHALL BE HANDLED DIRECTLY BETWEEN BUYER AND SELLER. Prorations shall be made based on a 30-day month.

19. **WITHHOLDING TAXES:** Seller and Buyer agree to execute any instrument, affidavit, statement or instruction reasonably necessary to comply with federal (FIRPTA) and California withholding Law, if required (C.A.R. Forms AS and AB).

20. **MULTIPLE LISTING SERVICE ("MLS"):** Brokers are authorized to report to the MLS a pending sale and, upon Close Of Escrow, the terms of this transaction to be published and disseminated to persons and entities authorized to use the information on terms approved by the MLS.

21. **EQUAL HOUSING OPPORTUNITY:** The Property is sold in compliance with federal, state and local anti-discrimination Laws.

22. **ATTORNEY FEES:** In any action, proceeding, or arbitration between Buyer and Seller arising out of this Agreement, the prevailing Buyer or Seller shall be entitled to reasonable attorney fees and costs from the non-prevailing Buyer or Seller, except as provided in paragraph 17A.

23. **SELECTION OF SERVICE PROVIDERS:** If Brokers refer Buyer or Seller to persons, vendors, or service or product providers ("Providers"), Brokers do not guarantee the performance of any Providers. Buyer and Seller may select ANY Providers of their own choosing.

24. **TIME OF ESSENCE; ENTIRE CONTRACT; CHANGES:** Time is of the essence. All understandings between the parties are incorporated in this Agreement. Its terms are intended by the parties as a final, complete and exclusive expression of their Agreement with respect to its subject matter, and may not be contradicted by evidence of any prior agreement or contemporaneous oral agreement. If any provision of this Agreement is held to be ineffective or invalid, the remaining provisions will nevertheless be given full force and effect. **Neither this Agreement nor any provision in it may be extended, amended, modified, altered or changed, except in writing Signed by Buyer and Seller.**

25. **OTHER TERMS AND CONDITIONS,** including attached supplements:
   A. ☑ Buyer's Inspection Advisory (C.A.R. Form BIA)
   B. ☐ Purchase Agreement Addendum (C.A.R. Form PAA paragraph numbers: _____)
   C. ☐ Statewide Buyer and Seller Advisory (C.A.R. Form SBSA)
   D. _____
   _____

26. **DEFINITIONS:** As used in this Agreement:
   A. **"Acceptance"** means the time the offer or final counter offer is accepted in writing by a party and is delivered to and personally received by the other party or that party's authorized agent in accordance with the terms of this offer or a final counter offer.
   B. **"Agreement"** means the terms and conditions of this accepted California Residential Purchase Agreement and any accepted counter offers and addenda.
   C. **"C.A.R. Form"** means the specific form referenced or another comparable form agreed to by the parties.
   D. **"Close Of Escrow"** means the date the grant deed, or other evidence of transfer of title, is recorded. If the scheduled close of escrow falls on a Saturday, Sunday or legal holiday, then close of escrow shall be the next business day after the scheduled close of escrow date.
   E. **"Copy"** means copy by any means including photocopy, NCR, facsimile and electronic.
   F. **"Days"** means calendar days, unless otherwise required by Law.
   G. **"Days After"** means the specified number of calendar days after the occurrence of the event specified, not counting the calendar date on which the specified event occurs, and ending at 11:59PM on the final day.
   H. **"Days Prior"** means the specified number of calendar days before the occurrence of the event specified, not counting the calendar date on which the specified event is scheduled to occur.
   I. **"Electronic Copy" or "Electronic Signature"** means, as applicable, an electronic copy or signature complying with California Law. Buyer and Seller agree that electronic means will not be used by either party to modify or alter the content or integrity of this Agreement without the knowledge and consent of the other.
   J. **"Law"** means any law, code, statute, ordinance, regulation, rule or order, which is adopted by a controlling city, county, state or federal legislative, judicial or executive body or agency.
   K. **"Notice to Buyer to Perform"** means a document (C.A.R. Form NBP), which shall be in writing and Signed by Seller and shall give Buyer at least 24 hours **(or as otherwise specified in paragraph 14C(4))** to remove a contingency or perform as applicable.
   L. **"Repairs"** means any repairs (including pest control), alterations, replacements, modifications or retrofitting of the Property provided for under this Agreement.
   M. **"Signed"** means either a handwritten or electronic signature on an original document, Copy or any counterpart.
   N. **Singular and Plural** terms each include the other, when appropriate.

Buyer's Initials (_____)(_____)
Seller's Initials (_____)(_____)

Copyright © 1991-2004, CALIFORNIA ASSOCIATION OF REALTORS®, INC.
RPA-CA REVISED 10/02 (PAGE 6 OF 8)

Reviewed by _____ Date _____

EQUAL HOUSING OPPORTUNITY

CALIFORNIA RESIDENTIAL PURCHASE AGREEMENT (RPA-CA PAGE 6 OF 8)

Residential Purchase Agreement and Joint Escrow Instructions

Property Address: _____ Date: _____

27. AGENCY:

    A. DISCLOSURE: Buyer and Seller each acknowledge prior receipt of C.A.R. Form AD "Disclosure Regarding Real Estate Agency Relationships."

    B. POTENTIALLY COMPETING BUYERS AND SELLERS: Buyer and Seller each acknowledge receipt of a disclosure of the possibility of multiple representation by the Broker representing that principal. This disclosure may be part of a listing agreement, buyer-broker agreement or separate document (C.A.R. Form DA). Buyer understands that Broker representing Buyer may also represent other potential buyers, who may consider, make offers on or ultimately acquire the Property. Seller understands that Broker representing Seller may also represent other sellers with competing properties of interest to this Buyer.

    C. CONFIRMATION: The following agency relationships are hereby confirmed for this transaction:
Listing Agent _____ (Print Firm Name) is the agent of (check one): ☐ the Seller exclusively; or ☐ both the Buyer and Seller.
Selling Agent _____(Print Firm Name) (if not same as Listing Agent) is the agent of (check one): ☐ the Buyer exclusively; or ☐ the Seller exclusively; or ☐ both the Buyer and Seller. Real Estate Brokers are not parties to the Agreement between Buyer and Seller.

28. JOINT ESCROW INSTRUCTIONS TO ESCROW HOLDER:

    A. The following paragraphs, or applicable portions thereof, of this Agreement constitute the joint escrow instructions of Buyer and Seller to Escrow Holder, which Escrow Holder is to use along with any related counter offers and addenda, and any additional mutual instructions to close the escrow: 1, 2, 4, 12, 13B, 14E, 18, 19, 24, 25B and 25D, 26, 28, 29, 32A, 33 and paragraph D of the section titled Real Estate Brokers on page 8. If a Copy of the separate compensation agreement(s) provided for in paragraph 29 or 32A, or paragraph D of the section titled Real Estate Brokers on page 8 is deposited with Escrow Holder by Broker, Escrow Holder shall accept such agreement(s) and pay out from Buyer's or Seller's funds, as applicable, the Broker's compensation provided for in such agreement(s). The terms and conditions of this Agreement not set forth in the specified paragraphs are additional matters for the information of Escrow Holder, but about which Escrow Holder need not be concerned. Buyer and Seller will receive Escrow Holder's general provisions directly from Escrow Holder and will execute such provisions upon Escrow Holder's request. To the extent the general provisions are inconsistent or conflict with this Agreement, the general provisions will control as to the duties and obligations of Escrow Holder only. Buyer and Seller will execute additional instructions, documents and forms provided by Escrow Holder that are reasonably necessary to close the escrow.

    B. A Copy of this Agreement shall be delivered to Escrow Holder within **3** business days after Acceptance (or ☐ _____). Buyer and Seller authorize Escrow Holder to accept and rely on Copies and Signatures as defined in this Agreement as originals, to open escrow and for other purposes of escrow. The validity of this Agreement as between Buyer and Seller is not affected by whether or when Escrow Holder Signs this Agreement.

    C. Brokers are a party to the escrow for the sole purpose of compensation pursuant to paragraphs 29, 32A and paragraph D of the section titled Real Estate Brokers on page 8. Buyer and Seller irrevocably assign to Brokers compensation specified in paragraphs 29 and 32A, respectively, and irrevocably instruct Escrow Holder to disburse those funds to Brokers at Close Of Escrow or pursuant to any other mutually executed cancellation agreement. Compensation instructions can be amended or revoked only with the written consent of Brokers. Escrow Holder shall immediately notify Brokers: **(i)** if Buyer's initial or any additional deposit is not made pursuant to this Agreement, or is not good at time of deposit with Escrow Holder; or **(ii)** if Buyer and Seller instruct Escrow Holder to cancel escrow.

    D. A Copy of any amendment that affects any paragraph of this Agreement for which Escrow Holder is responsible shall be delivered to Escrow Holder within **2** business days after mutual execution of the amendment.

29. BROKER COMPENSATION FROM BUYER: If applicable, upon Close Of Escrow, **Buyer** agrees to pay compensation to Broker as specified in a separate written agreement between Buyer and Broker.

30. TERMS AND CONDITIONS OF OFFER:

This is an offer to purchase the Property on the above terms and conditions. All paragraphs with spaces for initials by Buyer and Seller are incorporated in this Agreement only if initialed by all parties. If at least one but not all parties initial, a counter offer is required until agreement is reached. Seller has the right to continue to offer the Property for sale and to accept any other offer at any time prior to notification of Acceptance. Buyer has read and acknowledges receipt of a Copy of the offer and agrees to the above confirmation of agency relationships. If this offer is accepted and Buyer subsequently defaults, Buyer may be responsible for payment of Brokers' compensation. This Agreement and any supplement, addendum or modification, including any Copy, may be Signed in two or more counterparts, all of which shall constitute one and the same writing.

Buyer's Initials (_____)(_____)
Seller's Initials (_____)(_____)

RPA-CA REVISED 10/02 (PAGE 7 OF 8)

Reviewed by _____ Date _____

CALIFORNIA RESIDENTIAL PURCHASE AGREEMENT (RPA-CA PAGE 7 OF 8)

Residential Purchase Agreement and Joint Escrow Instructions

Property Address: _____ Date: _____

31. EXPIRATION OF OFFER: This offer shall be deemed revoked and the deposit shall be returned unless the offer is Signed by Seller and a Copy of the Signed offer is personally received by Buyer, or by _____, who is authorized to receive it by 5:00 PM on the third calendar day after this offer is signed by Buyer (or, if checked, ☐ by _____ (date), at _____ AM/PM).

Date _____ Date _____

BUYER _____ BUYER _____

_____ _____
(Print name) **(Print name)**

_____
(Address)

32. BROKER COMPENSATION FROM SELLER:
    A. Upon Close Of Escrow, **Seller** agrees to pay compensation to Broker as specified in a separate written agreement between Seller and Broker.
    B. If escrow does not close, compensation is payable as specified in that separate written agreement.
33. ACCEPTANCE OF OFFER: Seller warrants that Seller is the owner of the Property, or has the authority to execute this Agreement. Seller accepts the above offer, agrees to sell the Property on the above terms and conditions, and agrees to the above confirmation of agency relationships. Seller has read and acknowledges receipt of a Copy of this Agreement, and authorizes Broker to deliver a Signed Copy to Buyer.
    ☐ (If checked) **SUBJECT TO ATTACHED COUNTER OFFER, DATED** _____.

Date _____ Date _____

SELLER _____ SELLER _____

_____ _____
(Print name) **(Print name)**

_____
(Address)

(___/___) **CONFIRMATION OF ACCEPTANCE:** A Copy of Signed Acceptance was personally received by Buyer or Buyer's authorized
(Initials) agent on (date) _____ at _____ AM/PM. **A binding Agreement is created when a Copy of Signed Acceptance is personally received by Buyer or Buyer's authorized agent whether or not confirmed in this document. Completion of this confirmation is not legally required in order to create a binding Agreement; it is solely intended to evidence the date that Confirmation of Acceptance has occurred.**

REAL ESTATE BROKERS:
A. Real Estate Brokers are not parties to the Agreement between Buyer and Seller.
B. Agency relationships are confirmed as stated in paragraph 27.
C. If specified in paragraph 2A, Agent who submitted the offer for Buyer acknowledges receipt of deposit.
D. **COOPERATING BROKER COMPENSATION:** Listing Broker agrees to pay Cooperating Broker **(Selling Firm)** and Cooperating Broker agrees to accept, out of Listing Broker's proceeds in escrow: **(i)** the amount specified in the MLS, provided Cooperating Broker is a Participant of the MLS in which the Property is offered for sale or a reciprocal MLS; or **(ii)** ☐ (if checked) the amount specified in a separate written agreement (C.A.R. Form CBC) between Listing Broker and Cooperating Broker.

Real Estate Broker (Selling Firm) _____
By _____ Date _____
Address _____ City _____ State _____ Zip _____
Telephone _____ Fax _____ E-mail _____

Real Estate Broker (Listing Firm) _____
By _____ Date _____
Address _____ City _____ State _____ Zip _____
Telephone _____ Fax _____ E-mail _____

ESCROW HOLDER ACKNOWLEDGMENT:
Escrow Holder acknowledges receipt of a Copy of this Agreement, (if checked, ☐ a deposit in the amount of $ _____), counter offer numbers _____ and _____, and agrees to act as Escrow Holder subject to paragraph 28 of this Agreement, any supplemental escrow instructions and the terms of Escrow Holder's general provisions.

Escrow Holder is advised that the date of Confirmation of Acceptance of the Agreement as between Buyer and Seller is _____

Escrow Holder _____ Escrow # _____
By _____ Date _____
Address _____
Phone/Fax/E-mail _____
Escrow Holder is licensed by the California Department of ☐ Corporations, ☐ Insurance, ☐ Real Estate. License # _____

(___/___) **REJECTION OF OFFER:** No counter offer is being made. This offer was reviewed and rejected by Seller on
(Seller's Initials) _____ (Date)

THIS FORM HAS BEEN APPROVED BY THE CALIFORNIA ASSOCIATION OF REALTORS® (C.A.R.). NO REPRESENTATION IS MADE AS TO THE LEGAL VALIDITY OR ADEQUACY OF ANY PROVISION IN ANY SPECIFIC TRANSACTION. A REAL ESTATE BROKER IS THE PERSON QUALIFIED TO ADVISE ON REAL ESTATE TRANSACTIONS. IF YOU DESIRE LEGAL OR TAX ADVICE, CONSULT AN APPROPRIATE PROFESSIONAL.

This form is available for use by the entire real estate industry. It is not intended to identify the user as a REALTOR®. REALTOR® is a registered collective membership mark which may be used only by members of the NATIONAL ASSOCIATION OF REALTORS® who subscribe to its Code of Ethics.

Published by the
California Association of REALTORS®

RPA-CA REVISED 10/02 (PAGE 8 OF 8)

Reviewed by _____ Date _____

CALIFORNIA RESIDENTIAL PURCHASE AGREEMENT (RPA-CA PAGE 8 OF 8)

Counter Offer

CALIFORNIA
ASSOCIATION
OF REALTORS®

COUNTER OFFER   No. _____
For use by Seller or Buyer. May be used for Multiple Counter Offer.
(C.A.R. Form CO, Revised 10/04)

Date _____, at _____, California.
This is a counter offer to the: ☐ California Residential Purchase Agreement, ☐ Counter Offer, or ☐ Other _____ ("Offer"),
dated _____, on property known as _____ ("Property"),
between _____ ("Buyer") and _____ ("Seller").
1. **TERMS:** The terms and conditions of the above referenced document are **accepted subject to the following:**
    A. **Paragraphs in the Offer that require initials by all parties, but are not initialed by all parties, are excluded from the final agreement unless specifically referenced for inclusion in paragraph 1C of this or another Counter Offer.**
    B. **Unless otherwise agreed in writing, down payment and loan amount(s) will be adjusted in the same proportion as in the original Offer.**
    C. _____
        _____
        _____
        _____
        _____
        _____

    D. The following attached supplements are incorporated into this Counter Offer: ☐ Addendum No.
        _____
        ☐ _____   ☐ _____
2. **RIGHT TO ACCEPT OTHER OFFERS:** Seller has the right to continue to offer the Property for sale or for other transaction, and to accept any other offer at any time prior to notification of acceptance, as described in paragraph 3. If this is a Seller Counter Offer, Seller's acceptance of another offer prior to Buyer's acceptance and communication of notification of this Counter Offer, shall revoke this Counter Offer.
3. **EXPIRATION:** This Counter Offer shall be deemed revoked and the deposits, if any, shall be returned unless this Counter Offer is signed by the Buyer or Seller to whom it is sent and a Copy of the signed Counter Offer is personally received by the person making this Counter Offer or _____,
    who is authorized to receive it, by 5:00PM on the third day after this Counter Offer is made or, (if checked)
    by ☐ _____ (date), at _____ AM/PM. This Counter Offer may be executed in counterparts.
4. ☐ **(If checked:) MULTIPLE COUNTER OFFER:** Seller is making a Counter Offer(s) to another prospective buyer(s) on terms that may or may not be the same as in this Counter Offer. Acceptance of this Counter Offer by Buyer shall **not** be binding unless and until it is subsequently re-Signed by Seller in paragraph 7 below and a Copy of the Counter Offer Signed in paragraph 7 is personally received by Buyer or by _____, who is authorized to receive it, by 5:00 PM on the third Day After this Counter Offer is made or, (if checked) by ☐ _____ (date), at _____ AM/PM. Prior to the completion of all of these events, Buyer and Seller shall have no duties or obligations for the purchase or sale of the Property.

5. **OFFER: BUYER OR SELLER MAKES THIS COUNTER OFFER ON THE TERMS ABOVE AND ACKNOWLEDGES RECEIPT OF A COPY.**
    _____   Date _____
    _____   Date _____
6. **ACCEPTANCE: I/WE** accept the above Counter Offer **(If checked ☐ SUBJECT TO THE ATTACHED COUNTER OFFER)** and acknowledge receipt of a Copy.
    _____   Date _____ Time _____ AM/PM
    _____   Date _____ Time _____ AM/PM
7. **MULTIPLE COUNTER OFFER SIGNATURE LINE: By signing below, Seller accepts this Multiple Counter Offer. NOTE TO SELLER: Do NOT sign in this box until after Buyer signs in paragraph 6. (Paragraph 7 applies only if paragraph 4 is checked.)**
    _____   Date _____ Time _____ **AM/PM**
    _____   Date _____ Time _____ **AM/PM**

8. (____ / ____) (Initials) **Confirmation of Acceptance:** A Copy of Signed Acceptance was personally received by the maker of the Counter Offer, or that person's authorized agent as specified in paragraph 3 (or, if this is a Multiple Counter Offer, the Buyer or Buyer's authorized agent as specified in paragraph 4) on (date) _____ at _____ AM/PM. **A binding Agreement is created when a Copy of Signed Acceptance is personally received by the maker of the Counter Offer, or that person's authorized agent (or, if this is a Multiple Counter Offer, the Buyer or Buyer's authorized agent) whether or not confirmed in this document. Completion of this confirmation is not legally required in order to create a binding Agreement; it is solely intended to evidence the date that Confirmation of Acceptance has occurred.**

SURE-TRAC
The System for Success®

Published and Distributed by:
REAL ESTATE BUSINESS SERVICES, INC.
a subsidiary of the California Association of REALTORS®
525 South Virgil Avenue, Los Angeles, California 90020

Reviewed by _____ Date _____

EQUAL HOUSING OPPORTUNITY

CO REVISED 10/04 (PAGE 1 OF 1)   Print Date

COUNTER OFFER (CO PAGE 1 OF 1)

CALIFORNIA
ASSOCIATION
OF REALTORS®

REQUEST FOR REPAIR No. _____
(Or Other Corrective Action)
(C.A.R. Form RR, Revised 10/02)

In accordance with the terms and conditions of the: ☐ California Residential Purchase Agreement or ☐ Other _____
_____ ("Agreement"), dated _____,
on property known as _____ ("Property"),
between _____ ("Buyer"),
and _____ ("Seller").

1. BUYER'S REQUEST:
   A. Buyer requests that Seller repair the following items or take the specified action prior to final verification of condition:
_____
_____
_____
_____
_____
_____
_____
_____

     ☐ See attached list dated _____ for requests.

   B. A copy of the following inspection or other report is attached.
     ☐ _____ ☐ _____
     ☐ _____ ☐ _____

Buyer _____ Date _____

Buyer _____ Date _____

2. SELLER'S RESPONSE TO BUYER'S REQUEST:
   A. If Buyer agrees to remove in writing the contingency(ies) identified on the attached Contingency Removal form (C.A.R. Form CR No. _____).
     (i) ☐ Seller agrees to repair or take the other specified action with respect to all of the items in 1A above.
   OR (ii) ☐ Seller agrees to repair or take the other specified action with respect to all of the items in 1A above, with the following
     exception(s): _____
_____
_____
_____
_____

   OR (iii) ☐ See attached response.
   B. ☐ Seller does not agree to any of Buyer's requests.

Seller _____ Date _____

Seller _____ Date _____

3. BUYER'S REPLY TO SELLER'S RESPONSE:
   A. ☐ Buyer accepts Seller's response, withdraws all requests for items that Seller has not agreed to, and removes the
     contingency(ies) identified in 2A above.
   B. ☐ Buyer withdraws the request in 1A above, and makes a new request as specified in the attached Request for Repair No. _____.

Buyer _____ Date _____

Buyer _____ Date _____

SURE TRAC
The System for Success®

Published and Distributed by:
REAL ESTATE BUSINESS SERVICES, INC.
a subsidiary of the California Association of REALTORS®
525 South Virgil Avenue, Los Angeles, California 90020

EQUAL HOUSING
OPPORTUNIT

RR REVISED 10/02 (PAGE 1 OF 1) Print Date

Reviewed by _____ Date _____

REQUEST FOR REPAIR (RR PAGE 1 OF 1)

HUD-1 Settlement Statement

A. Settlement Statement

U.S. Department of Housing
and Urban Development

OMB Approval No. 2502-0265
(expires 9/30/2006)

B. Type of Loan

				6. File Number:	7. Loan Number:	8. Mortgage Insurance Case Number:
1. ☐ FHA	2. ☐ FmHA	3. ☐ Conv. Unins.				
4. ☐ VA	5. ☐ Conv. Ins.					

C. Note: This form is furnished to give you a statement of actual settlement costs. Amounts paid to and by the settlement agent are shown. Items marked "(p.o.c.)" were paid outside the closing; they are shown here for informational purposes and are not included in the totals.

D. Name & Address of Borrower:	E. Name & Address of Seller:	F. Name & Address of Lender:

G. Property Location:	H. Settlement Agent:	
	Place of Settlement:	I. Settlement Date:

J. Summary of Borrower's Transaction		K. Summary of Seller's Transaction	
100. Gross Amount Due From Borrower		**400. Gross Amount Due To Seller**	
101. Contract sales price		401. Contract sales price	
102. Personal property		402. Personal property	
103. Settlement charges to borrower (line 1400)		403.	
104.		404.	
105.		405.	
Adjustments for items paid by seller in advance		**Adjustments for items paid by seller in advance**	
106. City/town taxes to		406. City/town taxes to	
107. County taxes to		407. County taxes to	
108. Assessments to		408. Assessments to	
109.		409.	
110.		410.	
111.		411.	
112.		412.	
120. Gross Amount Due From Borrower		**420. Gross Amount Due To Seller**	
200. Amounts Paid By Or In Behalf Of Borrower		**500. Reductions In Amount Due To Seller**	
201. Deposit or earnest money		501. Excess deposit (see instructions)	
202. Principal amount of new loan(s)		502. Settlement charges to seller (line 1400)	
203. Existing loan(s) taken subject to		503. Existing loan(s) taken subject to	
204.		504. Payoff of first mortgage loan	
205.		505. Payoff of second mortgage loan	
206.		506.	
207.		507.	
208.		508.	
209.		509.	
Adjustments for items unpaid by seller		**Adjustments for items unpaid by seller**	
210. City/town taxes to		510. City/town taxes to	
211. County taxes to		511. County taxes to	
212. Assessments to		512. Assessments to	
213.		513.	
214.		514.	
215.		515.	
216.		516.	
217.		517.	
218.		518.	
219.		519.	
220. Total Paid By/For Borrower		**520. Total Reduction Amount Due Seller**	
300. Cash At Settlement From/To Borrower		**600. Cash At Settlement To/From Seller**	
301. Gross Amount due from borrower (line 120)		601. Gross amount due to seller (line 420)	
302. Less amounts paid by/for borrower (line 220)	( )	602. Less reductions in amt. due seller (line 520)	( )
303. Cash ☐ From ☐ To Borrower		**603. Cash** ☐ To ☐ From Seller	

Section 5 of the Real Estate Settlement Procedures Act (RESPA) requires the following: • HUD must develop a Special Information Booklet to help persons borrowing money to finance the purchase of residential real estate to better understand the nature and costs of real estate settlement services; • Each lender must provide the booklet to all applicants from whom it receives or for whom it prepares a written application to borrow money to finance the purchase of residential real estate; • Lenders must prepare and distribute with the Booklet a Good Faith Estimate of the settlement costs that the borrower is likely to incur in connection with the settlement. These disclosures are manadatory.

Section 4(a) of RESPA mandates that HUD develop and prescribe this standard form to be used at the time of loan settlement to provide full disclosure of all charges imposed upon the borrower and seller. These are third party disclosures that are designed to provide the borrower with pertinent information during the settlement process in order to be a better shopper.

The Public Reporting Burden for this collection of information is estimated to average one hour per response, including the time for reviewing instructions, searching existing data sources, gathering and maintaining the data needed, and completing and reviewing the collection of information.

This agency may not collect this information, and you are not required to complete this form, unless it displays a currently valid OMB control number.

The information requested does not lend itself to confidentiality.

L. Settlement Charges

	Paid From Borrowers Funds at Settlement	Paid From Seller's Funds at Settlement
700. Total Sales/Broker's Commission based on price $ @ % =		
Division of Commission (line 700) as follows:		
701. $ to		
702. $ to		
703. Commission paid at Settlement		
704.		
800. Items Payable In Connection With Loan		
801. Loan Origination Fee %		
802. Loan Discount %		
803. Appraisal Fee to		
804. Credit Report to		
805. Lender's Inspection Fee		
806. Mortgage Insurance Application Fee to		
807. Assumption Fee		
808.		
809.		
810.		
811.		
900. Items Required By Lender To Be Paid In Advance		
901. Interest from to @$ /day		
902. Mortgage Insurance Premium for months to		
903. Hazard Insurance Premium for years to		
904. years to		
905.		
1000. Reserves Deposited With Lender		
1001. Hazard insurance months@$ per month		
1002. Mortgage insurance months@$ per month		
1003. City property taxes months@$ per month		
1004. County property taxes months@$ per month		
1005. Annual assessments months@$ per month		
1006. months@$ per month		
1007. months@$ per month		
1008. months@$ per month		
1100. Title Charges		
1101. Settlement or closing fee to		
1102. Abstract or title search to		
1103. Title examination to		
1104. Title insurance binder to		
1105. Document preparation to		
1106. Notary fees to		
1107. Attorney's fees to		
(includes above items numbers:)		
1108. Title insurance to		
(includes above items numbers:)		
1109. Lender's coverage $		
1110. Owner's coverage $		
1111.		
1112.		
1113.		
1200. Government Recording and Transfer Charges		
1201. Recording fees: Deed $; Mortgage $; Releases $		
1202. City/county tax/stamps: Deed $; Mortgage $		
1203. State tax/stamps: Deed $; Mortgage $		
1204.		
1205.		
1300. Additional Settlement Charges		
1301. Survey to		
1302. Pest inspection to		
1303.		
1304.		
1305.		
1400. Total Settlement Charges (enter on lines 103, Section J and 502, Section K)		

Understanding the HUD-1 Settlement Statement

Your offer has been accepted and it's time to close! Below is a line-by-line guide to the Settlement Statement from the folks who wrote it: The Department of Housing and Urban Development.[1] For additional information, please see the HUD website at www.hud.gov. You'll also find many of the terms used here in the Glossary beginning on page 179.

Section B

Check appropriate loan type and complete the remaining items as applicable.

Section C

This section provides a notice regarding settlement costs and requires no additional entry of information.

Sections D and E

Fill in the names and current mailing addresses and zip codes of the Borrower and the Seller. Where there is more than one Borrower or Seller, the name and address of each one is required. Use a supplementary page if needed to list multiple Borrowers or Sellers.

Section F

Fill in the name, current mailing address and zip code of the Lender.

Section G

The street address of the property being sold should be given. If there is no street address, a brief legal description or other location of the property should be inserted. In all cases give the zip code of the property.

Section H

Fill in name, address, and zip code of settlement agent; address and zip code of "place of settlement."

Section I

Date of settlement.

Section J

Summary of Borrower's Transaction. Line 101 is for the gross sales price of the property being sold, excluding the price of any items of tangible personal property if Borrower and Seller have agreed to a separate price for such items.

Line 102 is for the gross sales price of any items of tangible personal property excluded from Line 101. Personal property could include such items as carpets, drapes, stoves, refrigerators, etc. What constitutes personal property varies from state to state. Manufactured homes are not considered personal property for this purpose.

Line 103 is used to record the total charges to Borrower detailed in Section L and totaled on Line 1400.

Lines 104 and 105 are for additional amounts owed by the Borrower or items paid by the Seller prior to settlement but reimbursed by the Borrower at settlement. For example, the balance in the Seller's reserve account held in connection with an existing loan, if assigned to the Borrower in a loan assumption case, will be entered here. These lines will also be used when a tenant in the property being sold has not yet paid the rent, which the Borrower will collect, for a period of time prior to the settlement. The lines will also be used to indicate the treatment for any tenant security deposit. The Seller will be credited on Lines 404–405.

Lines 106 through 112 are for items which the Seller had paid in advance, and for which the Borrower must therefore reimburse the Seller. Examples of items for which adjustments will be made may include taxes and assessments paid in advance for an entire year or other period, when settlement occurs prior to the expiration of the year or other period for which they were paid. Additional examples include: flood and hazard insurance premiums, if the Borrower is being substituted as an insured under the same policy; mortgage insurance in loan assumption cases; planned unit development or condominium association assessments paid in advance; fuel or other supplies on hand, purchased by the Seller, which the Borrower will use when Borrower takes possession of the property; and ground rent paid in advance.

Line 120 is for the total of Lines 101 through 112.

Line 201 is for any amount paid against the sales price prior to settlement.

Line 202 is for the amount of the new loan made by the Lender or first user loan (a loan to finance construction of a new structure or purchase of manufactured home where the structure was constructed for sale or the manufactured home was purchased for purposes of resale and the loan is used as or converted to a loan to finance purchase by the first user).

For other loans covered by Regulation X, which finance construction of a new structure or purchase of a manufactured home, list the sales price of the land on Line 104, the construction cost or purchase price of manufactured home on Line 105 (Line 101 would be left blank in this instance) and amount of the loan on Line 202. The remainder of the form should be completed taking into account adjustments and charges related to the temporary financing and permanent financing and which are known at the date of settlement.

Line 203 is used for cases in which the Borrower is assuming or taking title subject to an existing loan or lien on the property.

Lines 204 – 209 are used for other items paid by or on behalf of the Borrower. Examples include cases in which the Seller has taken a trade-in or other property from the Borrower in part payment for the property being sold. They may also be used in cases in which a Seller (typically a builder) is making an "allowance" to the Borrower for carpets or drapes which the Borrower is to purchase separately. Lines 204–209 can also be used to indicate any Seller financing arrangements or other new loan not listed in Line 202. For example, if the Seller takes a note from the Borrower for part of the sales price, insert the principal amount of the note with a brief explanation on Lines 204–209.

Lines 210 through 219 are for items which have not yet been paid, and which the Borrower is expected to pay, but which are attributable in part to a period of time prior to the settlement. In jurisdictions in which taxes are paid late in the tax year, most cases will show the proration of taxes in these lines. Other examples include utilities used but not paid for by the Seller, rent collected in advance by the Seller from a tenant for a period extending beyond the settlement date, and interest on loan assumptions.

Line 220 is for the total of Lines 201 through 219.

Lines 301 and 302 are summary lines for the Borrower. Enter total in Line 120 on Line 301. Enter total in Line 220 on Line 302.

Line 303 may indicate either the cash required from the Borrower at settlement (the usual case in a purchase transaction) or cash payable to the Borrower at settlement (if, for example, the Borrower's deposit against the sales price, or earnest money, exceeded the Borrower's cash obligations in the transaction). Subtract Line 302 from Line 301 and enter the amount of cash due to or from the Borrower at settlement on Line 303. The appropriate box should be checked.

Section K

Summary of Seller's Transaction. Instructions for the use of Lines 101 and 102 and 104–112 above, apply also to Lines 401–412. Line 420 is for the total of Lines 401 through 412.

Line 501 is used if the Seller's real estate broker or other party who is not the settlement agent has received and holds the deposit against the sales price (earnest money) which exceeds the fee or commission owed to that party, and if that party will render the excess deposit directly to the Seller, rather than through the settlement agent, the amount of excess deposit should be entered on Line 501 and the amount of the total deposit (including commissions) should be entered on Line 201.

Line 502 is used to record the total charges to the Seller detailed in Section L and totaled on Line 1400.

Line 503 is used if the Borrower is assuming or taking title subject to existing liens which are to be deducted from sales price.

Lines 504 and 505 are used for the amounts (including any accrued interest) of any first and/or second loans which will be paid as part of the settlement.

Line 506 is used for deposits paid by the Borrower to the Seller or other party who is not the settlement agent. Enter the amount of the deposit in Line 201 on Line 506 unless Line 501 is used or the party who is not the settlement agent transfers all or part of the deposit to the settlement agent in which case the settlement agent will note in parentheses on Line 507 the amount of the deposit which is being disbursed as proceeds and enter in column for Line 506 the amount retained by the above described party for settlement services. If the settlement agent holds the deposit insert a note in Line 507 which indicates that the deposit is being disbursed as proceeds.

Lines 506 through 509 may be used to list additional liens which must be paid off through the settlement to clear title to the property. Other payoffs of Seller obligations should be shown on Lines 506–509 (but not on Lines 1303–1305). They may also be used to indicate funds to be held by the settlement agent for the payment of water, fuel, or other utility bills which cannot be prorated between the parties at settlement because the amounts used by the Seller prior to settlement are not yet known.

Subsequent disclosure of the actual amount of these post-settlement items to be paid from settlement funds is optional. Any amounts entered on Lines 204–209 including Seller financing arrangements should also be entered on Lines 506–509.

Instructions for the use of Lines 510 through 519 are the same as those for Lines 210 to 219 above.

Line 520 is for the total of Lines 501 through 519.

Lines 601 and 602 are summary lines for the Seller. Enter total in Line 420 on Line 610. Enter total in Line 520 on Line 602.

Line 603 may indicate either the cash required to be paid to the Seller at settlement (the usual case in a purchase transaction) or cash payable by the Seller at settlement. Subtract Line 602 from Line 601 and enter the amount of cash due to or from the Seller at settlement on Line 603. The appropriate box should be checked.

Section L Settlement Charges

For all items except those paid to and retained by the Lender, the name of the person or firm ultimately receiving the payment should be shown. In the case of "no cost" or "no point" loans, the charge to be paid by the lender to an affiliated or independent service provider should be shown as Paid Outside of Closing ("P.O.C.") and should not be used in computing totals. Such charges also include indirect payments or back-funded payments to mortgage brokers that arise from the settlement transaction. When used, "P.O.C." should be placed in the appropriate lines next to the identified item, not in the columns themselves.

Line 700 is used to enter the sales commission charged by the sales agent or broker. If the sales commission is based on a percentage of the price, enter the sales price, the percentage, and the dollar amount of the total commission paid by the Seller.

Lines 701 – 702 are to be used to state the split of the commission where the settlement agent disburses portions of the commission to two or more sales agents or brokers.

Line 703 is used to enter the amount of sales commission disbursed at settlement. If the sales agent or broker is retaining a part of the deposit against the sales price (earnest money) to apply towards the sales agent's or broker's commission, include in Line 703 only that part of the commission being disbursed at settlement and insert a note on Line 704 indicating the amount the sales agent or broker is retaining as a "P.O.C." item.

Line 704 may be used for additional charges made by the sales agent or broker, or for a sales commission charged to the Borrower, which will be disbursed by the settlement agent.

Line 801 is used to record the fee charged by the Lender for processing or originating the loan. If this fee is computed as a percentage of the loan amount, enter the percentage in the blank indicated.

Line 802 is used to record the loan discount or "points" charged by the Lender, and, if it is computed as a percentage of the loan amount, enter the percentage in the blank indicated.

Line 803 is used for appraisal fees if there is a separate charge for the appraisal. Appraisal fees for HUD and VA loans are also included on Line 803.

Line 804 is used for the cost of the credit report if there is a charge separate from the origination fee.

Line 805 is used only for inspections by the Lender or the Lender's agents. Charges for other pest or structural inspections required to be stated by these instructions should be entered in Lines 1301–1305.

Line 806 should be used for an application fee required by a private mortgage insurance company.

Line 807 is provided for convenience in using the form for loan assumption transactions.

Lines 808 – 811 are used to list additional items payable in connection with the loan including a CLO Access fee, a mortgage broker fee, fees for real estate property taxes or other real property charges.

Lines 901 – 905 This series is used to record the items which the Lender requires (but which are not necessarily paid to the lender, i.e., FHA mortgage insurance premium) to be paid at the time of settlement, other than reserves collected by the Lender and recorded in 1000 series.

Line 901 is used if interest is collected at settlement for a part of a month or other period between settlement and the date from which interest will be collected with the first regular monthly payment. Enter that amount here and include the per diem charges. If such interest is not collected until the first regular monthly payment, no entry should be made on Line 901.

Line 902 is used for mortgage insurance premiums due and payable at settlement, except reserves collected by the Lender and recorded in the 1000 series. A lump sum mortgage insurance premium paid at settlement should be inserted on Line 902, with a note that indicates that the premium is for the life of the loan.

Line 903 is used for hazard insurance premiums which the Lender requires to be paid at the time of settlement except reserves collected by the Lender and recorded in the 1000 series.

Lines 904 and 905 are used to list additional items required by the Lender (except for reserves collected by the Lender and recorded in the 1000 series) including flood insurance, mortgage life insurance, credit life insurance and disability insurance premiums. These lines are also used to list amounts paid at settlement for insurance not required by the Lender.

Lines 1000 – 1008 are used for amounts collected by the Lender from the Borrower and held in an account for the future payment of the obligations listed as they fall due. Include the time period (number of months) and the monthly assessment. In many jurisdictions this is referred to as an "escrow," "impound," or "trust" account. In addition to the items listed, some Lenders may require reserves for flood insurance, condominium owner's association assessments, etc.

After itemizing individual deposits in the 1000 series using single-item accounting, the servicer shall make an adjustment based on aggregate accounting. This adjustment equals the difference between the deposit required under aggregate accounting and the sum of the deposits required under single-item accounting. The computation steps for both accounting methods are set out in 3500.17(d). The adjustment will always be a negative number or zero (-0-). The settlement agent shall enter the aggregate adjustment amount on a final line in the 1000 series of the HUD-1 or HUD–1A statement.

During the phase-in period, as defined in 3500.17(b), an alternative procedure is available. If a servicer has not yet conducted the escrow account analysis to determine the aggregate accounting starting balance, the settlement agent may initially calculate the 1000 series deposits for the HUD-1 and HUD-1A settlement statement using single-item analysis with a one-month cushion (unless the mortgage loan documents indicate a smaller amount). In the escrow account analysis conducted within 45 days of settlement, the servicer shall adjust the escrow account to reflect the aggregate accounting balance.

Lines 1100 – 1113. This series covers title charges and charges by attorneys. The title charges include a variety of services performed by title companies or others and includes fees directly related to the transfer of title (title examination, title search, document preparation) and fees for title insurance. The legal charges include fees for Lender's, Seller's or Buyer's attorney, or the attorney preparing title work. The series also includes any fees for settlement or closing agents and notaries. In many jurisdictions the same person (for example, an attorney or a title insurance company) performs several of the services listed in this series and makes a single overall charge for such services. In such cases, enter the overall fee on Line 1107 (for attorneys), or Line 1108 (for title companies), and enter on that line the item numbers of the services listed which are covered in the overall fee. If this is done, no individual amounts need be entered into the borrower's and seller's columns for the individual items which are covered by the overall fee. In transactions involving more than one attorney, one attorney's fees should appear on Line 1107 and the other attorney's fees should be on Line 1111, 1112 or 1113. If an attorney is representing a buyer, seller, or lender and is also acting as a title agent, indicate on line 1107 which services are covered by the attorney fee and on line 1113 which services are covered by the insurance commission.

Line 1101 is used for the settlement agent's fee.

Lines 1102 and 1103 are used for the fees for the abstract or title search and title examination. In some jurisdictions the same person both searches the title (that is, performs the necessary research in the records) and examines title (that is, makes a determination as to what matters affect title, and provides a title report or opinion). If such a person charges only one fee for both services, it should be entered on Line 1103 unless the person performing these tasks is an attorney or a title company in which case the fees should be entered as described in the general directions for Lines 1100–1113. If separate persons perform these tasks, or if separate charges are made for searching and examination, they should be listed separately.

Line 1104 is used for the Title Insurance Binder which is also known as a commitment to insure.

Line 1105 is used for charges for preparation of deeds, mortgages, notes, etc. If more than one person receives a fee for such work in the same transaction, show the total paid in the appropriate column and the individual charges on the line following the word "to."

Line 1106 is used for the fee charged by a notary public for authenticating the execution of settlement documents.

Line 1107 is used to disclose the attorney's fees for the transaction. The instructions are discussed in the general directions for Lines 1100–1113. This line should include any charges by an attorney to represent a buyer, seller or lender in the real estate transaction.

Lines 1108 – 1110 are used for information regarding title insurance. Enter the total charge for title insurance (except for the cost of the title binder) on Line 1108. Enter on Lines 1109 and 1110 the individual charges for the Lender's and owner's policies. Note that these charges are not carried over into the Borrower's and Seller's columns, since to do so would result in a duplication of the amount in Line 1108. If a combination Lender's/owner's policy is purchased, show this amount as an additional entry on Lines 1109 and 1110.

Lines 1111 – 1113 are for the entry of other title charges not already itemized. Examples in some jurisdictions would include a fee to a private tax service, a fee to a county tax collector for a tax certificate, or a fee to a public title registrar for a certificate of title in a Torrens Act transaction. Line 1113 should be used to disclose services that are covered by the commission of an attorney acting as a title agent when Line 1107 is already being used to disclose the fees and services of the attorney in representing the buyer, seller, or lender in the real estate transaction.

Lines 1201 – 1205 are used for government recording and transfer charges. Recording and transfer charges should be itemized. Additional recording or transfer charges should be listed on Lines 1204 and 1205.

Lines 1301 and 1302 are used for fees for survey, pest inspection, radon inspection, lead-based paint inspection, or other similar inspections.

Lines 1303 – 1305 are used for any other settlement charges not referable to the categories listed above on the HUD-1, which are required to be stated by these instructions. Examples may include structural inspections or pre-sale inspection of heating, plumbing, or electrical equipment. These inspection charges may include a fee for insurance or warranty coverage.

Line 1400 is for the total settlement charges paid from Borrower's funds and Seller's funds. These totals are also entered on Lines 103 and 502, respectively, in sections J and K.

[1] *Source: The Department of Housing and Urban Development*

Mortgage Payment Tables

The tables on these pages show your monthly payment for varying loan amounts at different rates of interest.

15-Year Fixed-Rate Mortgage

$ Borrowed	4.00%	4.25%	4.50%	4.75%	5.00%	5.25%	5.500%	5.75%	6.00%
50000	369.84	376.14	382.50	388.92	395.40	401.94	408.54	415.21	421.93
100000	739.69	752.28	764.99	777.83	790.79	803.88	817.08	830.41	843.86
150000	1109.53	1128.42	1147.49	1166.75	1186.19	1205.82	1225.63	1245.62	1265.79
200000	1479.38	1504.56	1529.99	1555.66	1581.59	1607.76	1634.17	1660.82	1687.71
250000	1849.22	1880.70	1912.48	1944.58	1976.98	2009.69	2042.71	2076.03	2109.64
300000	2219.06	2256.84	2294.98	2333.50	2372.38	2411.63	2451.25	2491.23	2531.57
350000	2588.91	2632.97	2677.48	2722.41	2767.78	2813.57	2859.79	2906.44	2953.50
400000	2958.75	3009.11	3059.97	3111.33	3163.17	3215.51	3268.33	3321.64	3375.43
450000	3328.60	3385.25	3442.47	3500.24	3558.57	3617.45	3676.88	3736.85	3797.36
500000	3698.44	3761.39	3824.97	3889.16	3953.97	4019.39	4085.42	4152.05	4219.28
550000	4068.28	4137.53	4207.46	4278.08	4349.36	4421.33	4493.96	4567.26	4641.21
600000	4438.13	4513.67	4589.96	4666.99	4744.76	4823.27	4902.50	4982.46	5063.14
650000	4807.97	4889.81	4972.46	5055.91	5140.16	5225.21	5311.04	5397.67	5485.07
700000	5177.82	5265.95	5354.95	5444.82	5535.56	5627.14	5719.58	5812.87	5907.00
750000	5547.66	5642.09	5737.45	5833.74	5930.95	6029.08	6128.13	6228.08	6328.93
800000	5917.50	6018.23	6119.95	6222.66	6326.35	6431.02	6536.67	6643.28	6750.85
850000	6287.35	6394.37	6502.44	6611.57	6721.75	6832.96	6945.21	7058.49	7172.78
900000	6657.19	6770.51	6884.94	7000.49	7117.14	7234.90	7353.75	7473.69	7594.71
950000	7027.04	7146.64	7267.44	7389.40	7512.54	7636.84	7762.29	7888.90	8016.64
1000000	7396.88	7522.78	7649.93	7778.32	7907.94	8038.78	8170.83	8304.10	8438.57

15-Year Fixed-Rate Mortgage, continued

$ Borrowed	6.00%	6.25%	6.50%	6.75%	7.00%	7.25%	7.50%	7.75%	8.00%
50000	421.93	428.71	435.55	442.45	449.41	456.43	463.51	470.64	477.83
100000	843.86	857.42	871.11	884.91	898.83	912.86	927.01	941.28	955.65
150000	1265.79	1286.13	1306.66	1327.36	1348.24	1369.29	1390.52	1411.91	1433.48
200000	1687.71	1714.85	1742.21	1769.82	1797.66	1825.73	1854.02	1882.55	1911.30
250000	2109.64	2143.56	2177.77	2212.27	2247.07	2282.16	2317.53	2353.19	2389.13
300000	2531.57	2572.27	2613.32	2654.73	2696.48	2738.59	2781.04	2823.83	2866.96
350000	2953.50	3000.98	3048.88	3097.18	3145.90	3195.02	3244.54	3294.47	3344.78
400000	3375.43	3429.69	3484.43	3539.64	3595.31	3651.45	3708.05	3765.10	3822.61
450000	3797.36	3858.40	3919.98	3982.09	4044.73	4107.88	4171.56	4235.74	4300.43
500000	4219.28	4287.11	4355.54	4424.55	4494.14	4564.31	4635.06	4706.38	4778.26
550000	4641.21	4715.83	4791.09	4867.00	4943.56	5020.75	5098.57	5177.02	5256.09
600000	5063.14	5144.54	5226.64	5309.46	5392.97	5477.18	5562.07	5647.65	5733.91
650000	5485.07	5573.25	5662.20	5751.91	5842.38	5933.61	6025.58	6118.29	6211.74
700000	5907.00	6001.96	6097.75	6194.37	6291.80	6390.04	6489.09	6588.93	6689.56
750000	6328.93	6430.67	6533.31	6636.82	6741.21	6846.47	6952.59	7059.57	7167.39
800000	6750.85	6859.38	6968.86	7079.28	7190.63	7302.90	7416.10	7530.21	7645.22
850000	7172.78	7288.09	7404.41	7521.73	7640.04	7759.33	7879.61	8000.84	8123.04
900000	7594.71	7716.81	7839.97	7964.19	8089.45	8215.77	8343.11	8471.48	8600.87
950000	8016.64	8145.52	8275.52	8406.64	8538.87	8672.20	8806.62	8942.12	9078.69
1000000	8438.57	8574.23	8711.07	8849.09	8988.28	9128.63	9270.12	9412.76	9556.52

15-Year Fixed-Rate Mortgage, continued

$ Borrowed	8.00%	8.25%	8.50%	8.75%	9.00%	9.25%	9.50%	9.75%	10.00%
50000	477.83	485.07	492.37	499.72	507.13	514.60	522.11	529.68	537.30
100000	955.65	970.14	984.74	999.45	1014.27	1029.19	1044.22	1059.36	1074.61
150000	1433.48	1455.21	1477.11	1499.17	1521.40	1543.79	1566.34	1589.04	1611.91
200000	1911.30	1940.28	1969.48	1998.90	2028.53	2058.38	2088.45	2118.73	2149.21
250000	2389.13	2425.35	2461.85	2498.62	2535.67	2572.98	2610.56	2648.41	2686.51
300000	2866.96	2910.42	2954.22	2998.35	3042.80	3087.58	3132.67	3178.09	3223.82
350000	3344.78	3395.49	3446.59	3498.07	3549.93	3602.17	3654.79	3707.77	3761.12
400000	3822.61	3880.56	3938.96	3997.79	4057.07	4116.77	4176.90	4237.45	4298.42
450000	4300.43	4365.63	4431.33	4497.52	4564.20	4631.37	4699.01	4767.13	4835.72
500000	4778.26	4850.70	4923.70	4997.24	5071.33	5145.96	5221.12	5296.81	5373.03
550000	5256.09	5335.77	5416.07	5496.97	5578.47	5660.56	5743.24	5826.49	5910.33
600000	5733.91	5820.84	5908.44	5996.69	6085.60	6175.15	6265.35	6356.18	6447.63
650000	6211.74	6305.91	6400.81	6496.42	6592.73	6689.75	6787.46	6885.86	6984.93
700000	6689.56	6790.98	6893.18	6996.14	7099.87	7204.35	7309.57	7415.54	7522.24
750000	7167.39	7276.05	7385.55	7495.86	7607.00	7718.94	7831.69	7945.22	8059.54
800000	7645.22	7761.12	7877.92	7995.59	8114.13	8233.54	8353.80	8474.90	8596.84
850000	8123.04	8246.19	8370.29	8495.31	8621.27	8748.13	8875.91	9004.58	9134.14
900000	8600.87	8731.26	8862.66	8995.04	9128.40	9262.73	9398.02	9534.26	9671.45
950000	9078.69	9216.33	9355.03	9494.76	9635.53	9777.33	9920.13	10063.95	10208.75
1000000	9556.52	9701.40	9847.40	9994.49	10142.67	10291.92	10442.25	10593.63	10746.05

30-Year Fixed-Rate Mortgage

$ Borrowed	4.00%	4.25%	4.50%	4.75%	5.00%	5.25%	5.50%	5.75%	6.00%
50000	238.71	245.97	253.34	260.82	268.41	276.10	283.89	291.79	299.78
100000	477.42	491.94	506.69	521.65	536.82	552.20	567.79	583.57	599.55
150000	716.12	737.91	760.03	782.47	805.23	828.31	851.68	875.36	899.33
200000	954.83	983.88	1013.37	1043.29	1073.64	1104.41	1135.58	1167.15	1199.10
250000	1193.54	1229.85	1266.71	1304.12	1342.05	1380.51	1419.47	1458.93	1498.88
300000	1432.25	1475.82	1520.06	1564.94	1610.46	1656.61	1703.37	1750.72	1798.65
350000	1670.95	1721.79	1773.40	1825.77	1878.88	1932.71	1987.26	2042.50	2098.43
400000	1909.66	1967.76	2026.74	2086.59	2147.29	2208.81	2271.16	2334.29	2398.20
450000	2148.37	2213.73	2280.08	2347.41	2415.70	2484.92	2555.05	2626.08	2697.98
500000	2387.08	2459.70	2533.43	2608.24	2684.11	2761.02	2838.95	2917.86	2997.75
550000	2625.78	2705.67	2786.77	2869.06	2952.52	3037.12	3122.84	3209.65	3297.53
600000	2864.49	2951.64	3040.11	3129.88	3220.93	3313.22	3406.73	3501.44	3597.30
650000	3103.20	3197.61	3293.45	3390.71	3489.34	3589.32	3690.63	3793.22	3897.08
700000	3341.91	3443.58	3546.80	3651.53	3757.75	3865.43	3974.52	4085.01	4196.85
750000	3580.61	3689.55	3800.14	3912.36	4026.16	4141.53	4258.42	4376.80	4496.63
800000	3819.32	3935.52	4053.48	4173.18	4294.57	4417.63	4542.31	4668.58	4796.40
850000	4058.03	4181.49	4306.83	4434.00	4562.98	4693.73	4826.21	4960.37	5096.18
900000	4296.74	4427.46	4560.17	4694.83	4831.39	4969.83	5110.10	5252.16	5395.95
950000	4535.45	4673.43	4813.51	4955.65	5099.81	5245.94	5394.00	5543.94	5695.73
1000000	4774.15	4919.40	5066.85	5216.47	5368.22	5522.04	5677.89	5835.73	5995.51

30-Year Fixed-Rate Mortgage, continued

$ Borrowed	6.00%	6.25%	6.50%	6.75%	7.00%	7.25%	7.50%	7.75%	8.00%
50000	299.78	307.86	316.03	324.30	332.65	341.09	349.61	358.21	366.88
100000	599.55	615.72	632.07	648.60	665.30	682.18	699.21	716.41	733.76
150000	899.33	923.58	948.10	972.90	997.95	1023.26	1048.82	1074.62	1100.65
200000	1199.10	1231.43	1264.14	1297.20	1330.60	1364.35	1398.43	1432.82	1467.53
250000	1498.88	1539.29	1580.17	1621.50	1663.26	1705.44	1748.04	1791.03	1834.41
300000	1798.65	1847.15	1896.20	1945.79	1995.91	2046.53	2097.64	2149.24	2201.29
350000	2098.43	2155.01	2212.24	2270.09	2328.56	2387.62	2447.25	2507.44	2568.18
400000	2398.20	2462.87	2528.27	2594.39	2661.21	2728.71	2796.86	2865.65	2935.06
450000	2697.98	2770.73	2844.31	2918.69	2993.86	3069.79	3146.47	3223.86	3301.94
500000	2997.75	3078.59	3160.34	3242.99	3326.51	3410.88	3496.07	3582.06	3668.82
550000	3297.53	3386.44	3476.37	3567.29	3659.16	3751.97	3845.68	3940.27	4035.71
600000	3597.30	3694.30	3792.41	3891.59	3991.81	4093.06	4195.29	4298.47	4402.59
650000	3897.08	4002.16	4108.44	4215.89	4324.47	4434.15	4544.89	4656.68	4769.47
700000	4196.85	4310.02	4424.48	4540.19	4657.12	4775.23	4894.50	5014.89	5136.35
750000	4496.63	4617.88	4740.51	4864.49	4989.77	5116.32	5244.11	5373.09	5503.23
800000	4796.40	4925.74	5056.54	5188.78	5322.42	5457.41	5593.72	5731.30	5870.12
850000	5096.18	5233.60	5372.58	5513.08	5655.07	5798.50	5943.32	6089.50	6237.00
900000	5395.95	5541.45	5688.61	5837.38	5987.72	6139.59	6292.93	6447.71	6603.88
950000	5695.73	5849.31	6004.65	6161.68	6320.37	6480.67	6642.54	6805.92	6970.76
1000000	5995.51	6157.17	6320.68	6485.98	6653.02	6821.76	6992.15	7164.12	7337.65

30-Year Fixed-Rate Mortgage, continued

$ Borrowed	8.00%	8.25%	8.50%	8.75%	9.00%	9.25%	9.50%	9.75%	10.00%
50000	366.88	375.63	384.46	393.35	402.31	411.34	420.43	429.58	438.79
100000	733.76	751.27	768.91	786.70	804.62	822.68	840.85	859.15	877.57
150000	1100.65	1126.90	1153.37	1180.05	1206.93	1234.01	1261.28	1288.73	1316.36
200000	1467.53	1502.53	1537.83	1573.40	1609.25	1645.35	1681.71	1718.31	1755.14
250000	1834.41	1878.17	1922.28	1966.75	2011.56	2056.69	2102.14	2147.89	2193.93
300000	2201.29	2253.80	2306.74	2360.10	2413.87	2468.03	2522.56	2577.46	2632.71
350000	2568.18	2629.43	2691.20	2753.45	2816.18	2879.36	2942.99	3007.04	3071.50
400000	2935.06	3005.07	3075.65	3146.80	3218.49	3290.70	3363.42	3436.62	3510.29
450000	3301.94	3380.70	3460.11	3540.15	3620.80	3702.04	3783.84	3866.19	3949.07
500000	3668.82	3756.33	3844.57	3933.50	4023.11	4113.38	4204.27	4295.77	4387.86
550000	4035.71	4131.97	4229.02	4326.85	4425.42	4524.71	4624.70	4725.35	4826.64
600000	4402.59	4507.60	4613.48	4720.20	4827.74	4936.05	5045.13	5154.93	5265.43
650000	4769.47	4883.23	4997.94	5113.55	5230.05	5347.39	5465.55	5584.50	5704.22
700000	5136.35	5258.87	5382.39	5506.90	5632.36	5758.73	5885.98	6014.08	6143.00
750000	5503.23	5634.50	5766.85	5900.25	6034.67	6170.07	6306.41	6443.66	6581.79
800000	5870.12	6010.13	6151.31	6293.60	6436.98	6581.40	6726.83	6873.24	7020.57
850000	6237.00	6385.77	6535.76	6686.95	6839.29	6992.74	7147.26	7302.81	7459.36
900000	6603.88	6761.40	6920.22	7080.30	7241.60	7404.08	7567.69	7732.39	7898.14
950000	6970.76	7137.03	7304.68	7473.65	7643.91	7815.42	7988.11	8161.97	8336.93
1000000	7337.65	7512.67	7689.13	7867.00	8046.23	8226.75	8408.54	8591.54	8775.72

Internet Resources

Government Agencies

Consumer Federation of America
www.consumerfed.org

Department of Housing & Urban Development (HUD)
www.hud.gov

Department of Veteran Affairs (VA)
www.va.gov
www.homeloansva.gov

Environmental Protection Agency Toxin Link
www.epa.gov/opptintr

Fannie Mae
www.FannieMae.com
www.HomePath.com

Federal Citizen Information Center
www.pueblo.gsa.gov

Federal Emergency Management Agency
www.fema.gov

Federal Reserve Board
www.federalreserve.gov

Federal Trade Commission
www.ftc.gov

Freddie Mac
www.FreddieMac.com

Ginnie Mae
www.ginniemae.gov

Home Information Center (Office of Affordable Housing)
www.ComCon.com

Trade Groups

American Society of Home Inspectors
www.ashi.com

Council of Better Business Bureaus
www.bbb.org

Mortgage Bankers Association
www.mbaa.com

National Association of Home Builders
www.nahb.org

National Association of Exclusive Buyer's Agents
www.naeba.com

National Association of Realtors
www.realtor.com

State Organizations

Alabama Housing
www.alabama.gov/living/housing.php

Alaska Housing Finance Corporation
www.ahfc.state.ak.us

Arizona Department of Real Estate
www.adre.org

Arkansas Real Estate Commission
state.ar.us/arec

California Housing Finance Agency
www.calhfa.ca.gov

Colorado Housing & Finance Authority
www.colohfa.org

Connecticut Housing Authority
www.chfa.org

Delaware State Housing Authority
www2.state.de.us/dsha

Florida Housing Finance Corporation
www.floridahousing.org

Georgia Department of Consumer Affairs—Housing
www.dca.state.ga.us/housing

Hawaii Housing & Community Development
www.hcdch.state.hi.us

Idaho Housing & Finance Association
www.ihfa.org

Illinois Housing Development Authority
www.ihda.org

Indiana Housing Finance Authority
www.in.gov/ihfa

Iowa Finance Authority
www.ifahome.com

Access Kansas—Housing
www.accesskansas.org/living/housing.html

Kentucky Housing Corporation
www.kyhousing.org

Maine Housing
www.maine.gov/portal/living/housing.html

Massachusetts
www.masshousing.com

Minnesota Housing Finance Agency
www.mhfa.state.mn.us

Mississippi Housing Commission
www.mshomecorp.com

Missouri Housing Development Corporation
www.mhdc.org

Montana
www.montana.gov

Nevada Department of Business & Industry—Housing
nvhousing.state.nv.us

New Hampshire Housing Finance Authority
www.nhhfa.org

New Jersey Housing & Mortgage Finance Agency
www.state.nj.us/dca/hmfa

New Mexico Mortgage Finance Authority
www.nmmfa.org

New York State Housing Finance Authority
www.nyhomes.org

North Carolina Housing Finance Authority
www.nchfa.org

North Dakota
www.discovernd.com/living

Ohio Housing Finance Agency
www.odod.ohio.gov/OHFA.htm

Oklahoma Housing Finance Agency
www.ohfa.org

Pennsylvania Housing Finance Agency
www.phfa.org

Rhode Island Housing & Mortgage Finance Corporation
www.rihousing.com

South Carolina State Housing Finance & Development Authority
www.sha.state.sc.us

South Dakota Housing Development Authority
www.sdhda.org

Texas Department of Housing & Community Affairs
www.tdhca.state.tx.us

Utah Housing Corporation
www.utahhousingcorp.org

Virginia Department of Housing & Community Development
www.dhcd.virginia.gov

Washington State Housing Finance Commission
www.wshfc.org

West Virginia Housing Development Fund
www.wvhdf.com

Wisconsin Housing & Economic Development Authority
www.wheda.com

Wyoming Community Development Authority
www.wyomingcda.com

About the Experts

Brian Yui, CEO HouseRebate.com

BRIAN YUI founded HouseRebate.com in 1999. HouseRebate.com is a full-service discount online/offline real estate brokerage firm with affiliates in all 50 states. Buyers are rewarded with a rebate of up to 1% of a home's purchase price and sellers can list their homes at discounted commission rates. A 2004 Inman Innovator Award finalist at the annual Real Estate Connect Conference, HouseRebate.com has been recognized as a company that embodies the spirit of innovation in the real estate industry.

Prior to founding HouseRebate.com, Yui was a senior executive for leading real estate companies such as Sunroad Enterprises and The Dermot Company.

He began his career at Coopers Lybrand (now PriceWaterhouse Coopers) as a Certified Public Accountant. Yui holds a M.B.T. degree from the University of Southern California and a B.S. degree from the University of California, Berkeley. He has been investing in residential real estate for 20 years. Yui is also a best-selling co-author of the book *Wake Up...Live the Life You Love: Purpose, Passion, Abundance.*

Visit HouseRebate.com at www.houserebate.com. Contact Brian Yui at 858.812.7875 or information@houserebate.com

Lori Shaw-Cohen, Writer and Editor

LORI SHAW-COHEN is an editor and nationally published free-lance journalist, whose work has appeared in numerous publications for almost three decades. Formerly the Managing Editor of 'TEEN magazine, Ms. Shaw-Cohen's parenting articles and columns, "The Parent Zone" and "Mom Central," have been featured regularly in major newspapers and regional magazines. Shaw-Cohen has appeared on television and radio and spoken at writers' conferences throughout the United States.

In 2004, Shaw-Cohen's nonfiction story, "Angel to the Bone," was published in the best-selling *Chicken Soup to Inspire the Body & Soul*. Originally from Southern California (by way of Manhattan), she moved to the Nashville area in 1996 with her husband and three children. Contact Lori Shaw-Cohen at ALoudVoice@aol.com.

Robert G. Allen, New York Times Best-Selling Author

ROBERT ALLEN, world-renowned mentor, author and speaker, has taught hundreds of thousands of people how to create their own wealth since the early '70s when he founded the concept of buying real estate with no money down.

His books include financial hardcovers that have broken records as the longest running New York Times Bestsellers, such as *Nothing Down, Creating Wealth, Multiple Streams of Income* and *Multiple Streams of Internet Income*. One of his recent books, *The One Minute Millionaire*, was co-authored by *Chicken Soup for the Soul* founder, Mark Victor Hansen.

If you are interested in real estate as a vehicle to create wealth, visit Robert Allen's website at www.multiplestreamsofincome.com or contact his business office at 801.852.8700.

Brian Tracy, Top-Selling Motivational Speaker and Author

BRIAN TRACY is Chairman and CEO of Brian Tracy International, a human resources company specializing in the training and development of individuals and organizations. Tracy is the best-

selling author of more than 30 books, including *Getting Rich Your Own Way* and *Million Dollar Habits*, and has written and produced more than 300 audio and video learning programs.

He speaks four languages and addresses more than 250,000 people each year. Tracy has lectured in 24 countries on the subjects of personal and professional development to corporate and public audiences, including the executives and staff of many of America's largest corporations.

To learn more about Brian Tracy visit www.briantracy.com, call 858.481.2977, email BrianTracy@briantracy.com or write to Brian Tracy International, 462 Stevens Ave., Suite 202, Solana Beach, CA, 92075.

William Emerson, CEO Quicken Loans

BILL EMERSON is the Chief Executive Officer of Quicken Loans, which is the largest online mortgage lender and one of the largest retail mortgage lenders in the U.S. He joined the company in 1993 and became vice president of Mortgage Operations before being promoted to CEO in February 2002.

Quicken Loans has been named to FORTUNE Magazine's list of the "100 Best Companies to Work For in America" and the company's website has been named a "Best of the Web" mortgage website by Forbes, Money and PC Magazines.

Visit www.quickenloans.com to apply for a mortgage or to access a variety of mortgage related tools such as calculators, articles and Quicken Loans' free Power Buyer Guide, a comprehensive resource for first-time home buyers.

Stewart Morris, Jr., President and CEO, Stewart Title Co.

STEWART MORRIS, JR. joined Stewart Title Co. in 1973 and was elected vice president in 1975. He became president of Stewart Title Co. and chairman of Stewart Title Guaranty Co. in 1991. Morris was elected advisory director of Stewart Information Services Corp. (NYSE-STC) in 1997 and to the board as president and co-chief officer in February 2000.

Morris often speaks at real estate conferences such as Title Tech, ALTA Technology Expo, RealConnect, Vision 2000, NAR Conference & Expo, ATIM and other industry forums, discussing technology, the real estate transaction process and e-commerce.

For additional information about the home selling and buying process, visit www.stewart.com or email Stewart Morris, Jr. at solutions@stewart.com.

Robert J. Bruss, Tax Specialist and Nationally Syndicated Real Estate Columnist

For 31 years, ROBERT BRUSS has written the weekly syndicated *"Real Estate Mailbag"* Q&A real estate column, the *"Real Estate Notebook"* feature on real estate trends, *"Real Estate Law and You"* about court decisions affecting real estate and *"Real Estate Book Review"* features.

Sometimes called the "Dear Abby of real estate," Bruss publishes two monthly newsletters, the *Robert Bruss Real Estate Law Newsletter* and the *Robert Bruss National Real Estate Newsletter*. He is the author of *The Smart Investor's Guide to Real Estate, The California Foreclosure Book—How to Earn Big Profits From California Foreclosure* and *Distressed Properties*.

Bruss is a California Real Estate attorney and a real estate broker as well as the former director of the National Association of Real Estate Editors. He is the winner of the 1997 Norman Woest Outstanding California Real Estate Educator Award. Visit the Bob Bruss Real Estate Center at www.bobbruss.com

Michael P. Fergus, President SIRVA Global Moving Services (Retired)

MICHAEL P. FERGUS, formerly president and Chief Executive Officer of Allied Van Lines, recently retired from his position as president of SIRVA Global Moving Services. SIRVA is a leader in providing relocation solutions to a diverse customer base around the world.

SIRVA conducts more than 365,000 relocations per year, transferring corporate and government employees and moving individual consumers. The company operates in more than 40 countries with approximately 8,000 employees and an extensive network of agents and other service providers.

For more information on SIRVA and additional tips on how to pack and move with children and pets, visit www.sirva.com.

Keith S. Fimian, Chairman and Founder, U.S. Inspect, LLC

KEITH S. FIMIAN is Chairman and Founder of U.S. Inspect, LLC, the nation's leading provider of property inspection services. The company operates in two principal segments, Residential Services and Corporate Services, providing customers and clients with nationwide coverage for more than 50 inspection types, including general home, termite, radon, mold, structural, private well, septic system, pool/hot tub and specialty inspection services.

From its headquarters in the suburbs of Washington, D.C., U.S. Inspect annually produces more than 120,000 inspection reports for clients involved in all facets of real estate. The inspection services company of choice for corporate America, U.S. Inspect has conducted well over a million property inspections. For more information call 888.874.6773 or visit www.usinspect.com.

Home Buying Glossary

A

Abstract of Title

A historical summary of a property's ownership and any other matters affecting the title.

Acceleration Clause

A provision in a mortgage that gives the lender the right to demand payment of the entire principal balance if any monthly payments are missed.

Acceptance

An offer's consent to enter into a contract and be bound by the terms of the offer.

Additional Principal Payment

A payment by a borrower of more than the scheduled principal amount due in order to reduce the remaining balance on the loan.

Adjustable-Rate Mortgage (ARM)

Also known as "variable-rate loans," ARMs usually offer a lower initial interest rate than fixed-rate loans. The interest rate fluctuates over the life of the loan based on market conditions, but the loan agreement generally sets maximum and minimum rates. When interest rates rise, generally so do your loan payments; when interest rates fall, your monthly payments may be lowered.

Adjusted Cost Basis

The cost of any improvements the seller makes to the property. Deducting the cost from the original sales price provides the profit or loss of a home when it is sold. See page 129 for more.

Adjustment Date

The date on which the interest rate changes for an adjustable-rate mortgage (ARM).

Agreement of Sale (Contract to Purchase or Purchase and Sale Agreement)

A contract in which the seller agrees to sell and the buyer agrees to buy a property for a certain price. The Agreement contains all the provisions and conditions for the purchase, must be in writing and signed by both parties.

Amortization

The gradual repayment of a mortgage loan by installments.

Amortization Schedule

A timetable for payment of a mortgage loan. An amortization schedule shows the amount of each payment applied to interest and principal and shows the remaining balance after each payment is made.

Annual Percentage Rate (APR)

The cost of a mortgage stated as a yearly rate. The APR includes the interest rate, points, broker fees, and certain other credit charges that the borrower is required to pay.

Application

A form used to apply for a mortgage loan and to record pertinent information concerning a prospective mortgagor and the proposed security.

Appraisal

A written analysis of the estimated value of a property prepared by a qualified appraiser. Differs from home inspection.

Appraised Value

An opinion of a property's fair market value, based on an appraiser's knowledge, experience, and analysis of the property.

Appraiser

A person qualified by education, training, and experience to estimate the value of property.

Appreciation

An increase in the value of a property due to changes in market conditions or other causes. The opposite of depreciation.

Assessed Value

The valuation placed on property by a public tax assessor for purposes of taxation.

Asset

Anything of monetary value that is owned by a person.

Assignment

The transfer of a mortgage from one person to another.

Assumable Mortgage

A mortgage that can be taken over ("assumed") by the buyer when the home is sold.

Assumption Clause

A provision in an assumable mortgage that allows a buyer to assume the mortgage from the seller. The loan does not need to be paid in full by the original borrower upon sale or transfer of the property.

Assumption Fee

The fee paid to a lender (usually by the purchaser of real property) resulting from the assumption of an existing mortgage.

B

Balance Sheet

A financial statement that shows assets, liabilities, and net worth as of a specific date.

Balloon Mortgage

A mortgage that has level monthly payments but provides for a lump sum payment to be due at the end of a specified term.

Bankruptcy

A proceeding in the federal courts in which a debtor, who owes more than his or her assets can repay, can relieve those debts by transferring his or her assets to a trustee. Bankruptcy may have serious consequences for the debtor's credit rating.

Beneficiary

The person designated to receive the income from a trust, estate, or a deed of trust.

Binder

A preliminary agreement secured by an earnest money deposit, in which a buyer offers to purchase real estate.

Blanket Insurance Policy

A single policy that covers more than one piece of property (or more than one person).

Bridge Loan (or Swing Loan)

A form of second trust that is collateralized or secured by the borrower's present home (which is usually for sale) allowing the proceeds to be used for closing on a new house before the present home is sold.

Broker

A person who, for a commission or a fee, brings parties together and assists in negotiating contracts between them. See Mortgage Broker.

Building Line (or Setback)

Guidelines limiting how close an owner can build to the street or an adjacent property.

Buydown Account

An account in which funds are held by the lender. These funds are applied to the monthly mortgage payment for the term of the initial buydown period, allowing for a lower mortgage payment.

Buydown Mortgage

A temporary buydown is a mortgage on which an initial lump sum payment is made by any party to reduce a borrower's monthly payments during the first few years of a mortgage. A permanent buydown reduces the interest rate over the entire life of a mortgage.

Buyer Broker (or Agent)

A real estate broker who exclusively represents the buyer's interests and whose commission is either paid by the buyer or through the seller or listing broker at closing.

C

Call Option

A provision in the mortgage that gives the lender the right to call the mortgage due and payable at the end of a specified period for any reason.

Cancellation Clause

A clause that details the conditions under which each party may terminate the agreement.

Cap

A provision of an adjustable-rate mortgage (ARM) that limits how much the interest rate or mortgage payments may increase or decrease.

Cash-Out Refinance

A refinance transaction in which the amount of money received from the new loan exceeds the total of the money needed to repay the existing mortgages, closing costs, points, and the amount required to satisfy any outstanding mortgage liens, allowing the borrower to receive additional cash that can be used for other purposes.

Certificate of Deposit

A document written by a bank or other financial institution that is evidence of a deposit, with the issuer's promise to return the deposit plus earnings at a specified interest rate within a set time period.

Certificate of Deposit Index

An index that is used to determine interest rate changes for certain ARM plans. See Adjustable-Rate Mortgage (ARM).

Certificate of Eligibility

A document issued by the Federal Government certifying a veteran's eligibility for a Department of Veterans Affairs (VA) mortgage.

Certificate of Reasonable Value

A document issued by the Department of Veterans Affairs (VA) that establishes the maximum value and loan amount for a VA mortgage.

Chain of Title

The history of all of the documents that transfer title to a parcel of real property, starting with the earliest existing document and ending with the most recent.

Change Frequency

The frequency (in months) of payment and/or interest rate changes in an adjustable-rate mortgage (ARM).

Clear Title

A title that is free of liens or legal questions of ownership of the property.

CLO Access Fee

Computer loan origination systems, or CLOs, are computer terminals sometimes available in real estate offices or other locations to help borrowers find the various types of loans offered by different lenders. The CLO operator may charge a fee for the services the CLO offers. This fee may be paid by the borrower or the lender.

Closing (or Settlement)

A meeting at which the sale of a property is finalized when the buyer signs the mortgage documents and pays the closing costs.

Closing Costs

Expenses incurred by buyers and sellers in transferring ownership of a property over and above the price of the property. Closing costs normally include an origination fee, attorneys' fee, taxes, an amount placed in escrow, and charges for obtaining title insurance and an inspection. The closing cost percentage will vary according to the area of the country.

Closing Statement

See HUD-1 Settlement Statement.

Cloud on Title

Any conditions revealed by a title search that adversely affect the title to real estate. Usually clouds on title cannot be removed except by curative measures such as a quitclaim deed, release, or court action.

Collateral

An asset (such as a car or a home) that guarantees the repayment of a loan. The borrower risks losing the asset if the loan is not repaid according to the terms of the contract.

Collection

The process used to bring a delinquent mortgage current and to file the necessary notices to proceed with foreclosure when necessary.

Co-Maker

A person who signs a promissory note along with the borrower. A co-maker's signature guarantees that the loan will be repaid, because the borrower and the co-maker are equally responsible for the repayment.

Commission

The fee charged by a broker or agent for negotiating a real estate or loan transaction. The commission fee is usually a percentage of the price of the property or loan.

Commitment Letter (or Loan Commitment)

A formal offer by the lender stating the terms under which it agrees to lend money to the home buyer.

Common Area Assessments

Levies against individual unit owners in a condominium or planned unit development (PUD) project for additional capital to defray Homeowner's Association costs and expenses and to repair, replace, maintain, improve, or operate the common areas of the project.

Common Areas

Those portions of a building, land, and amenities owned (or managed) by a planned unit development (PUD) or condominium project's Homeowner's Association that are used by all of the unit owners, who share in the common expenses of their operation and maintenance. Common areas include swimming pools, tennis courts and other recreational facilities, and common corridors of buildings, parking areas, etc.

Community Property

In some western and southwestern states, a form of ownership under which property acquired during a marriage is presumed to be owned jointly unless acquired as separate property by either spouse.

Comparable (or Comps)

An abbreviation for "comparable properties;" used for comparative purposes when assessing a home's worth. Comparables are properties like the property under consideration; they have reasonably the same size, location, amenities, and have recently been sold. Comparables help the appraiser to determine the approximate fair market value of the subject property.

Compound Interest

Interest paid on the original principal balance and on the accrued and unpaid interest.

Condemnation

The determination that a building is not fit for use or is dangerous and must be destroyed; the taking of private property for a public purpose through an exercise of the right of eminent domain.

Condominium

A real estate project in which each unit owner has title to a unit in a building, undivided interest in the common areas of the project, and sometimes the exclusive use of certain limited common areas.

Condominium Conversion

Changing the ownership of an existing building (usually a rental project) to the condominium form of ownership.

Construction Loan

A short-term, interim loan for financing the cost of construction. The lender makes payments to the builder at periodic intervals as the work progresses.

Consumer Reporting Agency (or Bureau)

An organization that prepares reports that are used by lenders to determine a potential borrower's credit history.

Contingency

A condition that must be met before a contract is legally binding. For example, home purchasers often include a contingency specifying that the contract is not binding until the purchaser obtains a satisfactory home inspection report from a qualified home inspector.

Contract

An oral or written agreement to do or to not do a certain thing.

Conventional Mortgage

A mortgage that is not insured or guaranteed by the federal government.

Convertibility Clause

A provision in some adjustable-rate mortgages (ARMs) that allows the borrower to change the ARM to a fixed-rate mortgage at specified timeframes after loan origination.

Convertible ARM

An adjustable-rate mortgage (ARM) that can be converted to a fixed-rate mortgage under specified conditions.

Cooperative (Co-Op)

A type of multiple ownership in which the residents of a multi-unit housing complex own shares in the cooperative corporation that owns the property, giving each resident the right to occupy a specific apartment or unit.

Co-Signer

A second party who signs a promissory note and takes responsibility for a debt.

Counter Offer

A new offer that varies the price and/or terms of the original offer and rejects the terms of that original offer.

Covenant

A legal assurance or promise in a deed or other document, or implied by the law.

Covenants, Conditions & Restrictions (CC&Rs)

Rules and regulations for a housing development or community, such as acceptable landscaping or improvements that can be made to individual units.

Credit

An agreement in which a borrower receives something of value in exchange or a promise to repay the lender at a later date.

Credit History

A record of an individual's open and fully repaid debts.

Creditor

A person to whom money is owed.

Credit Report

A report of an individual's credit history prepared by a credit bureau and used by a lender in determining the loan applicant's creditworthiness.

D

Debt
An amount owed to another. See Installment Loan.

Declaration of Restrictions
A set of restrictions filed by a subdivider to cover an entire tract or subdivision.

Deed
The legal document conveying title to a property.

Deed-In-Lieu (or Voluntary Conveyance)
A deed given by a mortgagor to the mortgagee to satisfy a debt and avoid foreclosure.

Deed Of Trust
The document used in some states instead of a mortgage; title is conveyed to a trustee.

Default
Failure to comply with the requirements of a mortgage.

Delinquency
Failure to make mortgage payments when they are due.

Deposit
A sum of money given to bind the sale of real estate, or a sum of money given to ensure payment or an advance of funds in the processing of a loan. See Earnest Money Deposit.

Depreciation
A decline in the value of a property; the opposite of appreciation.

Down Payment
The part of the purchase price of a property that the buyer pays in cash and does not finance with a mortgage.

Dual Agency
A relationship in which a real estate agent or broker represents both parties in a transaction.

Due-On-Sale Provision
A provision in a mortgage that allows the lender to demand repayment in full if the borrower sells the property that serves as security for the mortgage.

E

Earnest Money Deposit
A deposit made by the potential home buyer to show that he or she is serious about buying the house.

Easement
A right of way giving people other than the owner access to or through a property.

Eminent Domain
The right of a government to take private property for public use upon payment of its fair market value. The basis for condemnation proceedings.

Encroachment
An improvement that intrudes illegally onto another's property.

Encumbrance

Anything that affects or limits the title to a property, such as mortgages, leases, easements, or restrictions.

Endorser

A person who signs his or her ownership interest over to another party.

Equal Credit Opportunity Act (ECOA)

A federal law that requires lenders and other creditors to make credit equally available without discrimination based on race, color, religion, national origin, age, sex, marital status, or receipt of income from public assistance programs.

Equity

A homeowner's financial interest in a property. Equity is the difference between the fair market value of the property and the amount still owed on its mortgage(s).

Escrow

The holding of money or documents by a neutral third party prior to closing. It can also be an account held by the lender (or servicer) into which a homeowner pays money for taxes and insurance.

Escrow Account

A trust account held in the borrower's name to pay obligations such as property taxes and insurance premiums.

Escrow Analysis

The periodic examination of an escrow account to determine if current monthly deposits will be sufficient to pay taxes, insurance, and other bills when due.

Escrow Payment

The portion of a mortgagor's monthly payment that is held by the servicer to pay for taxes, hazard insurance, mortgage insurance, lease payments, and other items as they become due. Known as "impounds" or "reserves" in some states.

Estate

The ownership interest of an individual in real property. The sum total of all the real property and personal property owned by an individual at time of death.

Eviction

The lawful expulsion of an occupant from real property.

Examination of Title

The report on the title of a property from the public records.

F

Fair Housing Act

Landmark federal law passed in 1965 and amended in 1988 that makes it illegal to deny rent or refuse to sell to anyone based on race, color, religion, sex or national origin. The 1988 amendment expanded the protections to include family status and disability.

Fair Market Value

Potential sale price for a piece of property if it were sold on the open market. Comparable sales of similar properties in the area are used by real estate appraisers to determine the fair market value. Differences in quality and size of the property are added or deducted from comparable sales prices.

Fannie Mae

Fannie Mae, or The Federal National Mortgage Association, is a congressionally chartered, shareholder-owned company that buys mortgages from lenders and resells them as securities on the secondary mortgage market.

Fiduciary Duty

The relationship of trust that buyers and sellers expect from a real estate agent who is obliged to act in the beneficiary's best interest.

First Mortgage

The primary mortgage on a property that has priority over all other voluntary liens.

Fixed-Rate Loan

A loan that usually has repayment terms of 15, 20, or 30 years. Both the interest rate and the monthly payments (for principal and interest) stay the same during the life of the loan.

Flat Fee

A set fee charged by a broker instead of a commission.

Foreclosure

The legal process reserved by a lender to terminate the borrower's interest in a property after a loan has been defaulted. When the process is completed, the lender may sell the property and keep the proceeds to satisfy its mortgage and any legal costs. Any excess proceeds may be used to satisfy other liens or be returned to the borrower.

Freddie Mac

The common name for the Federal Home Loan Mortgage Corporation, a congressionally chartered institution that buys mortgages from lenders and resells them as securities on the secondary mortgage market.

G

Ginnie Mae

The popular name for the Government National Mortgage Association. Ginnie Mae is a government-owned agency which buys mortgages from lending institutions, securitizes them, and then sells them to investors. Because the payments to investors are guaranteed by the full faith and credit of the U.S. Government, they return slightly less interest than other mortgage-backed securities.

Good Faith Estimate

An estimate from an institutional lender that shows the costs a borrower will incur, including loan-processing charges and inspection fees.

Government Mortgage (or Guaranteed Loan)

A mortgage that is insured by the Federal Housing Administration (FHA) or guaranteed by the Department of Veterans Affairs (VA) or the Rural Housing Service (RHS).

Grantee

The person to whom an interest in real property is conveyed.

Graduated Payment Mortgage

A mortgage that requires a borrower to make larger monthly payments over the term of the loan. The payment is unusually low for the first few years but gradually rises until year three or five, then remains fixed.

Grantor

The person conveying an interest in real property.

H

Hazard Insurance
Insurance coverage that compensates for physical damage to a property from fire, wind, vandalism, or other hazards.

Holdback
A contract provision stating that money will be withheld until a certain condition is satisfied.

Home Equity Line of Credit (HELOC)
A mortgage loan, secured by equity in the borrower's home, allowing the borrower to obtain multiple advances on the load proceeds at his or her discretion, usually through a check book or credit card.

Home Inspection
A thorough inspection that evaluates the structural and mechanical condition of a property.

Home Warranty
A type of insurance that covers repairs to certain parts of a house and some fixtures.

Homeowner's Association (HOA)
A nonprofit association that manages the common areas of a planned unit development (PUD) or condominium project. In the case of a condominium project, the Homeowner's Association has no ownership interest in the common elements. In a PUD project, the Homeowner's Association holds title to the common elements.

Homeowner's Insurance
An insurance policy that combines personal liability insurance and hazard insurance coverage for a dwelling and its contents.

Housing Expense Ratio
The percentage of gross monthly income that goes toward paying housing expenses.

Housing & Urban Development, Department of (HUD)
U.S. Government Agency whose mission is to increase home ownership, support community development and increase access to affordable housing free from discrimination.

HUD-1 Settlement Statement
A document that provides an itemized listing of the funds that are payable at closing. Items that appear on this statement include real estate commissions, loan fee points, and initial escrow amounts. Each item on the statement is represented by a separate number within a standardized numbering system. The totals at the bottom of the HUD-1 Settlement Statement define the seller's net proceeds and buyer's net payment at closing. Also known as the "closing statement" or "settlement sheet."

I

Impounds
A portion of the monthly mortgage payment that is placed in an account and used to pay for hazard insurance, property taxes and private mortgage insurance.

Income Property
Real estate developed or improved to produce income from rent, etc.

Index

A number used to compute the interest rate for an adjustable-rate mortgage (ARM). The index is generally a published number or percentage, such as the average interest rate or yield on Treasury bills. A *margin* is added to the index to determine the interest rate that will be charged on the ARM. This interest rate is subject to any caps that are associated with the mortgage.

Individual Retirement Account (IRA)

A retirement account that allows individuals to make tax-deferred contributions to a personal retirement fund.

Initial Interest Rate

The original interest rate of the mortgage at the time of closing. Sometimes known as "start rate" or "teaser."

Installment

The regular periodic payment that a borrower agrees to make to a lender.

Installment Loan

Borrowed money that is repaid in equal payments, known as "installments."

Insurance

A contract that provides compensation for specific losses in exchange for a periodic payment. An individual contract is known as an "insurance policy" and the periodic payment is known as an "insurance premium."

Insurance Holder

A document stating that insurance is temporarily in effect and will expire on a specified date.

Insured Mortgage

A mortgage that is protected by the Federal Housing Administration (FHA) or by private mortgage insurance (PMI). If the borrower defaults on the loan, the insurer must pay the lender the lesser of the loss incurred or the insured amount.

Interest

The fee charged for borrowing money.

Interest Accrual Rate

The percentage rate at which interest accrues on the mortgage. In most cases, it is also the rate used to calculate the monthly payments.

Interest-Only Mortgage

A loan in which the borrower pays only the interest that accrues on the loan balance each month. Because each payment goes toward interest, the outstanding balance of the loan does not decline with each payment.

Interest Rate

The rate of interest in effect for monthly payment due.

Interest Rate Buydown Plan

An arrangement wherein the property seller (or any other party) deposits money into an account so that it can be released each month to reduce the mortgagor's monthly payments during the early years of a mortgage.

Interest Rate Ceiling

For an adjustable-rate mortgage (ARM), the maximum interest rate, as specified in the mortgage note.

Interest Rate Floor

For an adjustable-rate mortgage (ARM), the minimum interest rate, as specified in the mortgage note.

Investment Property

A property that is not occupied by the owner.

J

Joint Tenancy
A form of co-ownership that gives each tenant equal rights in the property, including the right of survivorship.

Judgment
A decision made by a court of law.

Judgment Lien
A lien on the property of a debtor resulting from the decree of a court, usually involving repayment of a debt to a creditor.

Jumbo Loan
A loan that exceeds Fannie Mae's legislated mortgage amount limits.

L

Lease
A written agreement between the property owner and a commercial or residential tenant stipulating the conditions under which the tenant may possess the real estate for a specified period of time and rent.

Leasehold Estate
A way of holding title to a property in which the mortgagor does not actually own the property but rather has a recorded long-term lease on it.

Lease Option
A lease that contains the right to purchase the property for a specific price within a certain time frame.

Lease Purchase Mortgage Loan
An alternative financing option that allows for low- and moderate-income home buyers to lease a home from a nonprofit organization with an option to buy. Each month's rent payment consists of principal, interest, taxes, and insurance (PITI) payments on the first mortgage plus an extra amount that is earmarked for deposit into a savings account in which money for a down payment will accrue.

Legal Description
A property description recognized by law that is sufficient to locate and identify the property without oral testimony.

Liabilities
A person's financial obligations. Liabilities include long- and short-term debt, as well as any other amounts that are owed to others.

Liability Insurance
Insurance coverage that offers protection against claims alleging that a property owner's negligence or inappropriate action resulted in bodily injury or property damage to another party.

Lien
A legal claim against a property that must be paid off when property is sold.

Lifetime Payment Cap
For an adjustable-rate mortgage (ARM), a limit on the amount that payments can increase or decrease over the life of the mortgage.

Lifetime Rate Cap
For an adjustable-rate mortgage (ARM), a limit on the amount that the interest rate can increase or decrease over the life of the loan.

Line Of Credit
An agreement by a commercial bank or other financial institution to extend credit up to a certain amount for a certain time to a specified borrower.

Listing
A piece of property placed on the market by a listing agent.

Loan
A sum of borrowed money (principal) that is generally repaid with interest.

Loan Origination Fees
Fees charged by the lender for processing the loan and are often expressed as a percentage of the loan amount.

Loan Commitment
See Commitment Letter.

Loan-to-Value (LTV) Percentage
The relationship between the principal balance of the mortgage and the appraised value (or sales price if it is lower) of the property. For example, a $100,000 home with an $80,000 mortgage has a LTV percentage of 80%.

Lock-In
A written agreement in which the lender guarantees a specified interest rate if a mortgage goes to closing within a set period of time. The lock-in also usually specifies the number of points to be paid at closing.

Lock-In Period
The time period during which the lender has guaranteed an interest rate to a borrower.

M

Maintenance Fee
The monthly assessment paid by Homeowner's Association members for the repair and maintenance of common areas.

Margin
For an adjustable-rate mortgage (ARM), the amount that is added to the index to establish the interest rate on each adjustment date, subject to any limitations on the interest rate change.

Master-Planned Community
A suburban plan that includes homes and commercial, work, educational, and community facilities.

Maturity
The date on which the principal balance of a loan, bond, or other financial instrument becomes due and payable.

Maximum Financing
A mortgage amount that is within 5% of the highest loan-to-value (LTV) percentage allowed for a specific program. Maximum financing on a fixed-rate mortgage would be 90%† or higher, because 95% is the maximum allowable LTV percentage for that program.

Merged Credit Report
A credit report that contains information from three credit repositories.

Modification
Changing the terms of a mortgage.

Money Market Account

A savings account that provides bank depositors with many of the advantages of a money market fund. Certain regulatory restrictions apply to the withdrawal of funds from a money market account.

Money Market Fund

A mutual fund that allows individuals to participate in managed investments in short-term debt securities, such as certificates of deposit and Treasury bills.

Monthly Fixed Installment

That portion of the total monthly payment that is applied toward principal and interest. When a mortgage negatively amortizes, the monthly fixed installment does not include any amount for principal reduction.

Monthly Payment Mortgage

A mortgage that requires payments to reduce the debt once a month.

Mortgage

A legal document that pledges a property to the lender as security for payment of a debt.

Mortgage Banker

A company that originates mortgages exclusively for resale in the secondary mortgage market.

Mortgage Broker

An individual or company that brings borrowers and lenders together for the purpose of loan origination. Mortgage brokers typically require a fee or a commission for their services.

Mortgagee

The lender in a mortgage agreement.

Mortgage Insurance

A contract that insures the lender against loss caused by a mortgagor's default on a government mortgage or conventional mortgage. Mortgage insurance can be issued by a private company or by a government agency such as the Federal Housing Administration (FHA). Depending on the type of mortgage insurance, the insurance may cover a percentage of or virtually the entire mortgage loan. See Private Mortgage Insurance (PMI).

Mortgage Insurance Premium (MIP)

The amount paid by a mortgagor for mortgage insurance, either to a government agency such as Federal Housing Administration (FHA) or to a private mortgage insurance (PMI) company.

Mortgage Life Insurance

A type of term life insurance often bought by mortgagors. The amount of coverage decreases as the principal balance declines. In the event that the borrower dies while the policy is in force, the debt is automatically satisfied by insurance proceeds.

Mortgagor

The borrower in a mortgage agreement.

Multiple Listing Service (MLS)

A service that combines listings of all available homes in an area into one directory or database, with the exception of For Sale By Owner (FSBO) properties.

N

Negative Amortization
A gradual increase in mortgage debt that occurs when the monthly payment is not large enough to cover the entire principal and interest due. The amount of the shortfall is added to the remaining balance to create "negative" amortization.

Net Cash Flow
The income that remains for an investment property after the monthly operating income is reduced by the monthly housing expense, which includes principal, interest, taxes, and insurance (PITI) for the mortgage, Homeowner's Association dues, leasehold payments, and subordinate financing payments.

Net Worth
The value of all of a person's assets, including cash, minus all liabilities.

No Cash-Out Refinance
A refinance transaction where the new mortgage amount is limited to the sum of the remaining balance of the existing first mortgage, closing costs (including pre-paid items), points, the amount required to satisfy any mortgage liens that are more than one year old (if the borrower chooses to satisfy them), and others funds for the borrower's use (as long as the amount does not exceed 1% of the principal amount of the new mortgage).

Non-Liquid Asset
An asset that cannot be easily converted into cash.

Note
A legal document that obligates a borrower to repay a mortgage loan at a stated interest rate during a specified period of time.

Note Rate
The interest rate stated on a mortgage note.

Notice of Default
A formal written notice to a borrower that his or her loan is in default and that legal action may be taken.

Novation
A release of liability to the first borrower of a loan, and the substitution of a another borrower with the lender's approval.

O

Option
A situation in which a buyer puts down money for the right to purchase a piece of real estate within a set time period but does not have an obligation to buy.

Original Principal Balance
The total amount of principal owed on a mortgage before any payments are made.

Origination Fee
A fee paid to originator of the loan. The origination fee is stated in the form of points. A point is 1% of the mortgage amount.

Owner Financing
A property purchase transaction in which the property seller provides all or part of the financing.

P

Payment Change Date
The date when a new monthly payment amount takes effect on an adjustable-rate (ARM), or a graduated-payment adjustable period.

Periodic Payment Cap
For an adjustable-rate mortgage (ARM), a limit on the amount that the interest payment can increase or decrease during any one adjustment period.

Periodic Rate Cap
For an adjustable-rate mortgage (ARM), a limit on the amount that the interest rate can increase or decrease during any one adjustment period, regardless of how high or low the index might be.

PITI Reserves
A cash amount that a borrower must have on hand after making a down payment and paying all closing costs for the purchase of a home. The principal, interest taxes, and insurance (PITI) reserves must equal the amount that the borrower would have to pay for PITI for a predefined number of months.

Planned Unit Development (PUD)
A project or subdivision that includes common property that is owned and maintained by a Homeowner's Association for the benefit and use of the individual PUD unit owners.

Point
One-time charge by the lender for originating a loan. A point is 1% of the amount of the mortgage.

Possession
When a buyer signs the papers and receives the keys to the house, he or she officially takes possession.

Power of Attorney
A legal document that authorizes one person to act on another's behalf. A power of attorney can grant complete authority or can be limited to certain acts and certain periods of time.

Prepaid Interest
Interest paid before it is due. Frequently, at the close of a real estate transaction borrowers will pay for the interest on their loan that falls between the closing period and the first monthly payment.

Prepayment
Any amount paid to reduce the principal balance of a loan before the due date.

Prepayment Penalty
A fee that may be charged to a borrower who pays off a loan before it is due.

Pre-Qualification
The process of determining how much a prospective home buyer will be eligible to borrow before he or she applies for a loan.

Prime Rate
The interest rate that banks charge to their preferred customers. Changes in the prime rate influence changes in other rates, including mortgage interest rates.

Principal
The amount borrowed or remaining unpaid. The part of the monthly payment that reduces the remaining balance of a mortgage.

Principal, Interest, Taxes, and Insurance (PITI)

The four components of a monthly mortgage payment. Principal refers to the part of the monthly payment that reduces the remaining balance of the mortgage. Interest is the fee charged for borrowing money. Taxes and insurance refer to the amounts that are paid into an escrow account each month for property taxes, mortgage insurance, and hazard insurance.

Private Mortgage Insurance (PMI)

Mortgage insurance that is provided by a private mortgage insurance company to protect lenders against loss if a borrower defaults. Most lenders generally require PMI for a loan with loan-to-value (LTV) percentage in excess of 80%.

Promissory Note

A written promise to repay a specified amount over a specified period of time.

Proration

Agreed upon percentages of certain expenses associated with a piece of property that must be paid by the buyer or the seller at the time of closing.

Purchase Agreement

A document that details the purchase price and conditions of the transaction.

Purchase Money Transaction

The acquisition of property through the payment of money or its equivalent.

Q

Qualifying Ratios

Calculations that are used in determining whether a borrower can qualify for a mortgage. Qualifying ratios are based on two separate calculations: housing expense as a percentage of income ratio and total debt obligations as a percentage of income.

Quitclaim Deed

A deed that transfers without warranty whatever interest or title a grantor may have at the time the conveyance is made.

R

Rate-Lock

A commitment issued by the lender to a borrower or other mortgage originator guaranteeing a specified interest rate for a specified period of time.

Real Estate

Land and anything permanently affixed to it, including buildings.

Real Estate Agent

A real estate agent has a state license to represent a buyer or a seller in a real estate transaction in exchange for a commission. Unless they are also brokers, agents must work in association with a real estate broker or brokerage company.

Real Estate Attorney

A lawyer specializing in real estate transactions.

Real Estate Broker

A real estate agent who is licensed by the state to represent a buyer or seller in a real estate transaction in exchange for a commission. Most brokers also have agents working for them, and are entitled to a portion of their commissions.

Real Estate Settlement Procedures Act (RESPA)

A federal law designed to make sellers and buyers aware of settlement fees and other transaction-related costs. RESPA also outlaws kickbacks in the real estate business.

Real Property

Land and anything permanently affixed to it, including buildings.

Realtor

A real estate broker or an associate who holds active membership in a local real estate board that is affiliated with the National Association of Realtors.

Recession

The cancellation or annulment of a transaction or contract by the operation of a law or by mutual consent. Borrowers usually have the option to cancel a refinance transaction within three business days after it has closed.

Recording

The noting in the registrar's office of the details of a properly executed legal document, such as a deed, a mortgage note, a satisfaction of mortgage, or an extension of mortgage, making it a part of the public record.

Refinance Transaction

The process of paying off one loan with the proceeds from a new loan using the same property as security.

Regulation Z

A federal code issued under the Truth in Lending Act that requires a borrower to be advised in writing of all costs associated with the credit portion of a financial transaction.

Rehabilitation Mortgage

A mortgage created to cover the costs of repairing, improving, and sometimes acquiring an existing property.

Rent with Option to Buy

See Lease Option.

Repayment Plan

An arrangement made to repay delinquent installments or advances. Lenders' formal repayment plans are called "relief provisions."

Reserve Fund

Money set aside by a Homeowner's Association for major repairs or improvements.

Reverse Exchange

A reverse exchange is a type of tax-deferred exchange in which a replacement property is purchased prior to closing on the sale of the relinquished property.

Reverse Mortgage

A special type of loan available to equity-rich owners. Repayment is not necessary until the borrower sells the property.

Right of First Refusal

A provision in an agreement that requires the owner of a property to give another party the first opportunity to purchase or lease the property before he or she offers it for sale or lease to others.

Right of Ingress or Egress

The right to enter or leave a designated premise.

Right of Survivorship

In joint tenancy, the right of survivors to acquire the interest of a deceased joint tenant.

Right of Way

The right to pass over or use another's land.

S

Sale-Leaseback

A transaction in which the buyer leases back the property to the seller for an agreed upon period of time.

Second Mortgage

A mortgage that has a lien position subordinate to the first mortgage.

Secondary Mortgage Market

The buying and selling of an existing mortgage.

Secured Loan

A loan that is backed by collateral.

Security

The property that will be pledged as collateral for a loan.

Seller Broker (or Agent)

A seller broker represents the interest of the seller.

Servicer

An organization that collects principal and interest payments from borrowers and manages borrowers' escrow accounts. The servicer often services mortgages that have been purchased by an investor in the secondary mortgage market.

Settlement Sheet

See HUD-1 Settlement Statement.

Standard Payment Calculation

The method used to determine the monthly payment required to repay the remaining balance of the mortgage at the current interest rate.

Subdivision

A housing development that is created by dividing a tract of land into individual lots for sale or lease.

Subordinate Financing

Any mortgage or lien with a priority lower than that of the first mortgage.

Survey

A drawing or map showing the precise legal boundaries of a property, the location of improvements, easements, rights of way, encroachments, and other physical features.

Sweat Equity

Contribution to the construction or rehabilitation of a property using labor or services rather than cash.

T

Tax Lien
A lien placed against a property for nonpayment of taxes.

Tenancy by the Entirety
A type of joint tenancy in a property that provides right of survivorship and is available only to the husband and wife.

Tenancy in Common
A type of joint tenancy in a property without right of survivorship.

Thrift Institution
A general term for savings banks and savings and loan associations.

Title
A legal document proving a person's right to or ownership of a property.

Title Company
A company that specializes in examining and insuring titles to real estate.

Title Insurance
Insurance that protects the lender or the buyer against loss arising from disputes over ownership of a property.

Title Search
A check of the title records to ensure that the seller is the legal owner of the property and that there are no liens or other claims outstanding.

Torrens Act Transaction
A legal system for the registration of land used to verify the ownership and encumbrances (except tax liens), without the necessity of an additional search of the public records. The Torrens Act has been adopted in about 10 states. The purpose pertaining to registration of title to land is to conclusively establish an indefeasible title.

Total Expense Ratio
Total obligations as a percentage of gross monthly income. The total expense ratio includes monthly housing expenses plus other monthly debts.

Trade Equity
Equity that results from a property purchaser giving his or her existing property (or an asset other than real estate) as trade for all or part of the down payment for the property that is being purchased.

Transfer of Ownership
Any means by which the ownership of property changes hands. Lenders consider all of the following situations to be a transfer of ownership: the purchase of a property "subject to" the mortgage, the assumption of the mortgage debt by the property purchaser, and any exchange of possession of the property under a land sales contract or any other land trust device.

Transfer Tax
State or local tax payable when title passes from one owner to another.

Treasury Index
An index that is used to determine interest rate changes for certain adjustable-rate mortgage (ARM) plans.

Truth In Lending

A federal law that requires lenders to fully disclose, in writing, the terms and conditions of a mortgage, including the annual percentage rate (APR) and other charges.

Two to Four Family Property

A property that consists of a structure that provides living space (dwelling units) for two to four families, although ownership of the structure is evidenced by a single deed.

Trustee

A fiduciary who holds or controls property for the benefit of another.

U

Underwriting

The process of evaluating a loan application to determine the risk involved for the lender. Underwriting involves an analysis of the borrower's creditworthiness and the quality of the property itself.

Unsecured Loan

A loan that is not backed by collateral.

V

VA Mortgage

A mortgage that is guaranteed by the Department of Veterans Affairs (VA), also known as a "government mortgage."

Value Range Pricing

In some areas of the country, homes are listed for sale at a range between two prices as opposed to a fixed price.

Variable-Interest Rate

A loan rate that moves up and down based on factors including changes in the rate paid on bank certificates of deposit or Treasury bills.

Vested

Having the right to use a portion of a fund as an individual retirement fund.

W

What-if Scenario

A change in the amount that is used as the basis of an affordability analysis. What-if scenarios can include changes to monthly income, debt, or down payment funds, or to the qualifying ratios or down payment expenses that are used in the analysis.

Wraparound Mortgage

A refinanced home loan in which the balances on all mortgages are combined into one loan.

Index

L

M

N

O

P

R

S

Credits

Quick Order Form

Telephone orders: Call toll-free, 888.248.6222.

Email orders: orders@quantumleaves.com

Mail orders: Quantum Leaves Publishing℠
P.O. Box 429, Del Mar, CA 92014

✄ -

Please send more FREE information on:

❑ **Private Labeling**   ❑ **Speaking/Seminars**   ❑ **Consulting**

Name: _____

Address: _____

City: _____ **State:** _____ **Zip:** _____

Telephone: _____

Email: _____

Please send me _____ copies of *Home Buying by the Experts*.™

Price per book: $14.95 plus 7.75% sales tax for California residents

U.S. Shipping: $6.95 for the first book and $2.00 for each additional book

International: $10.00 for the first book and $5.00 for each additional book

Payment: ❑ Check ❑ Visa/MC

Card number: _____

Name on card: _____ **Exp.:** _____

Code (from back of Visa/MC) _____

As a Special Free Bonus to Readers

Receive a 12-month subscription to our e-newsletter designed to keep you up to date on home buying news, trends, mortgage programs and much more.

Sign up today at
www.homebuyingbytheexperts.com